First World War
and Army of Occupation
War Diary
France, Belgium and Germany

GUARDS DIVISION
1 Guards Brigade
Headquarters
1 March 1917 - 30 March 1917

WO95/1213/6

The Naval & Military Press Ltd
www.nmarchive.com
Published in association with The National Archives

Published by

The Naval & Military Press Ltd

Unit 10 Ridgewood Industrial Park,

Uckfield, East Sussex,

TN22 5QE England

Tel: +44 (0) 1825 749494

www.naval-military-press.com

www.nmarchive.com

This diary has been reprinted in facsimile from the original. Any imperfections are inevitably reproduced and the quality may fall short of modern type and cartographic standards.

© **Crown Copyright**
Images reproduced by permission of The National Archives, London, England, 2015.

Contents

Document type	Place/Title	Date From	Date To
Heading	WO95/1213 Mar 1917.		
War Diary	Billon Camps	01/03/1917	10/03/1917
War Diary	Billon Wood	05/03/1917	13/03/1917
War Diary	Billon Wood To T.17.d.5.4.	13/03/1917	15/03/1917
War Diary	T.17.d.5.4	15/03/1917	18/03/1917
War Diary	T.17.d.5.4 to U.19.a.8.8	19/03/1917	19/03/1917
War Diary	U.19.a.8.8	20/03/1917	22/03/1917
War Diary	U.19.a.8.8 To Bois Douage	23/03/1917	23/03/1917
War Diary	Bois Douage	24/03/1917	26/03/1917
War Diary	Arrow Head Copse	27/03/1917	30/03/1917
Operation(al) Order(s)	1st Guards Brigade Order No. 104.	09/03/1917	09/03/1917
Miscellaneous	March Table		
Operation(al) Order(s)	Amendment to 1st Guards Brigade Order No. 104.	11/03/1917	11/03/1917
Operation(al) Order(s)	1st Guards Brigade Warning Order No. 105.	13/03/1917	13/03/1917
Miscellaneous	1st G.B. No. 1940/3.		
Miscellaneous	1st Guards Brigade Defence Scheme (Provisional) Saillisel Sector.	12/03/1917	12/03/1917
Miscellaneous	Appendix "B". Disposition On Machine Guns.		
Miscellaneous	Appendix "D". Medical Arrangements.		
Map	Scale. 1/10000		
Diagram etc			
Operation(al) Order(s)	1st Guards Brigade Order No. 104.	09/03/1917	09/03/1917
Miscellaneous	March Table		
Miscellaneous	1st G.B. No. 1940/3.	18/03/1917	18/03/1917
Miscellaneous	1st Guards Brigade Defence Scheme (Provisional) Saillisel Sector.	12/03/1917	12/03/1917
Miscellaneous	Appendix "B". Disposition On Machine Guns		
Miscellaneous	Appendix "D". Medical Arrangements.		
Diagram etc	M. 109/4.		
Diagram etc	Scale 1/20000		
Miscellaneous	1st Guards Brigade Intelligence Report. 8 a.m. Mch. 13th to 8 a.m. Mch. 14th.	13/03/1917	13/03/1917
Miscellaneous	1st G. B.No. 117.	26/03/1917	26/03/1917
Miscellaneous	1st G.B. No. 1940.	11/03/1917	11/03/1917
Miscellaneous	Instructions No. 2 for Saillisel Sector.	11/03/1917	11/03/1917
Miscellaneous	1st Guards Brigade Intelligence Report. 8 a.m. Mch. 13th to 8 a.m. Mch. 14th.	13/03/1917	13/03/1917
Operation(al) Order(s)	1st Guards Brigade Commanding Order No. 106.	14/03/1917	14/03/1917
Operation(al) Order(s)	1st Guards Brigade Order No. 107.	17/03/1917	17/03/1917
Operation(al) Order(s)	In Continuation Of 1st Guards Brigade Order No. 107	17/03/1917	17/03/1917
Operation(al) Order(s)	1st Guards Brigade Operation Order No. 107	17/03/1917	17/03/1917
Operation(al) Order(s)	1st Guards Brigade Operation Order No. 108	18/03/1917	18/03/1917
Operation(al) Order(s)	1st Guards Brigade Operation Order No. 109.	19/03/1917	19/03/1917
Operation(al) Order(s)	1st Guards Brigade Operation Order No. 108. App. 342.	18/03/1917	18/03/1917
Operation(al) Order(s)	1st Guards Brigade Operation Order No. 109. App. 343.	19/03/1917	19/03/1917
Operation(al) Order(s)	1st Guards Brigade Operation Order No. 110. App. 344.	19/03/1917	19/03/1917
Operation(al) Order(s)	1st Guards Brigade Operation Order No. 110	19/03/1917	19/03/1917

Operation(al) Order(s)	1st Guards Brigade Operation Order No. 111.	20/03/1917	20/03/1917
Operation(al) Order(s)	1st Guards Brigade Operation Order No. 111. App. 345.	20/03/1917	20/03/1917
Operation(al) Order(s)	1st Guards Brigade Operation Order No. 112. App. 346.	21/03/1917	21/03/1917
Miscellaneous	1st G.B. No. 38.	20/03/1917	20/03/1917
Operation(al) Order(s)	1st Guards Brigade Warning Order No. 112.	21/03/1917	21/03/1917
Operation(al) Order(s)	1st Guards Brigade Operation Order No. 113. App. 347.	21/03/1917	21/03/1917
Miscellaneous	Appendix "E"		
Operation(al) Order(s)	1st Guards Brigade Operation Order No. 113.	21/03/1917	21/03/1917
Miscellaneous	Appendix "E"		
Operation(al) Order(s)	1st Guards Brigade Order No. 114. App. 348.	22/03/1917	22/03/1917
Miscellaneous	1st G.B. No. 59.	22/03/1917	22/03/1917
Operation(al) Order(s)	1st Guards Brigade Operation Order No. 115. App. 350.	22/03/1917	22/03/1917
Operation(al) Order(s)	1st Guards Brigade Operation Order No. 115.	22/03/1917	22/03/1917
Miscellaneous	Notes On A Conference Held At Brigade H.Q., 30 Th March 1917	30/03/1917	30/03/1917
Diagram etc	Table Of Trench ?		
Miscellaneous	1st G.B. No. 119.	26/03/1917	26/03/1917
Miscellaneous	1st G.B. No. 117.	26/03/1917	26/03/1917

co 95
12:13
New libi

WAR DIARY or INTELLIGENCE SUMMARY

Army Form C. 2118.

Vol 20

Headquarters, 1st Guards Bde.

March 1917.

Place	Date	Hour	Summary of Events and Information	Remarks and references to Appendices
WIZERNES Camp	March 1st 2nd 3rd		Bde was employed daily in washing — drill parades — fatigues etc. Pole Bayonet fighting courses started — On March 2nd 3rd Bn exhibition moved from MILLE to RINTY Camp 15.	(A 335)
	4th	14.30am	The Major General addressed all officers after church on the subject of open warfare — He laid stress on the use of the compass forcibly. He urged all ranks to get out of their heads the idea of moving from one line of trenches to another in mass.	
	5th to 10th		During this week a large amount of training in open warfare was carried out. The formation to be adopted in the event of a German retirement — an advance from our front line was chiefly practiced — A scout class under Major the Hon W. R. Bailey D.S.O. 2nd Bn Grenadier Gds was formed & carried out training during this period. 3rd Bn was employed on them every day. Three fatigues were numerous & one Bn was employed on them for 3 days — A lecture on Court Martial was given by the D.A.A.G 3rd Army & another the 3rd Bn Bde.	

WAR DIARY or INTELLIGENCE SUMMARY

Army Form C. 2118.

(Erase heading not required.)

Place	Date	Hour	Summary of Events and Information	Remarks and references to Appendices
BILLON WOOD	March 5th to 10th 18		1st Guards Bde Order No 104 was issued on March 9th. A conference was held at Div H.Q. at 3pm on March 10th	App 336
	March 11th		Church services as usual in the morning. 2nd Coldstream moved to FRÉGICOURT area.	
	12th to 14th		1st Irish Gds moved to FRÉGICOURT area. 2nd Coldstream relieved 2nd Scots Gds in left subsector SAILLISEL sector. MG Bde 2nd G.Coy & T.M.Bty relieved 3rd Gds Bde 2nd G.Coy & T.M.Bty in the line. 1st Gds Bde Provisional Defence Scheme issued.	App 337
	March 15th		Conference at Div H.Q. As every indication pointed to an enemy withdrawal the Major General pointed out that to the objective, they could be attacked to the Rode in attempting the principles on which the advance would be carried out. He outlined the F. Ser training order No 105 issued. 1st Irish Gds relieved 4th Gren Gds in right subsector. 3rd Bn Coldstream Gds relieved 2nd Bn Coldstream Gds moved into support. Casualties: 2nd Coldstream Gds - 2/Lt V.M.Reilly wounded - OR Killed 3. Wounded 14	App 338

WAR DIARY or INTELLIGENCE SUMMARY

Army Form C. 2118.

Place	Date	Hour	Summary of Events and Information	Remarks and references to Appendices
BILLON (WOOD) to T.17.d.5.4.	2nd Sept 23	5 pm	Bde H.Q. moved from BILLON Wood to T.17.d.5.4. 1st Bn. Bde learning orders 105 issued.	Appx 340
	2nd & 3rd	12 noon	Casualties. 2nd Coldm Gds 1 O.R. killed 1 wounded.	App 339
		6 pm	2nd B[atta]l[io]n Rifle Bde on our right reported enemy had evacuated his front line opposite their Rt B[attalio]n - & later that opposite their Left B[attalio]n.	Intelligence
		9.30 pm	1st Irish Gds reported that enemy front line opposite their left B[attalio]n vacated + was being occupied by our patrols.	Appx 341
		8 pm	2nd Gds Bde Order 106 issued.	
		12 noon	1st Irish Gds reported left front + any patrols had been able to enter enemy trenches.	
	3rd.0.5th	4 am	2nd Coldstream reported their right coy patrols able to enter enemy front line (M.1.2 Fray).	
		5.30 am	Orders received from Div that also 2nd Gds were to push forward at 10 a.m. Leading troops of adv. Bde went forward in accordance with 2nd Bde Order 106. The 3rd Rifle Brigade continued the advance, the [?] not M. Bde with 4 Gotha at first the enemy was pressing but soon the situation was definitely established as follows at noon. 1st Bn broke up right occupied extreme edge of SUZILICH Village with Rt Coy in the Desaurville + front Pl on right occupied eastern edge of BEYREATH Heath. 2nd Coldm occupied Gotha Trench with 2 coys + left front of BEYREATH Heath. 3rd Bn Rifle Brigade pushed forward to BARNHAWICK Trench.	Appx 341

WAR DIARY or INTELLIGENCE SUMMARY

Army Form C. 2118.

Place	Date	Hour	Summary of Events and Information	Remarks and references to Appendices
T.17.A.5.4.	2 March		Towards evening enemy shelling of SCHIESEL decreased, all relief resumed many fires during night 1/2 & 2/3. The line occupied by 8 1st Lincs & 2 W Yorks was consolidated as our front line. 1 section 8 2/6 south in 15 section in Libbing. Casualties up to 12 noon 1st Lincs Lt Col Burger D.S.O. Young wounded 2nd Coldstream Guards S.R. killed 2, wounded 21. O.R. knocked to.	

WAR DIARY or INTELLIGENCE SUMMARY

Army Form C. 2118.

(Erase heading not required.)

Place	Date	Hour	Summary of Events and Information	Remarks and references to Appendices
T.17.d.5.4.	17th		Advance continued. POZIERES retaken. POZE trench U.9 to X XX & BULGAR trench U.10 a. & FERDINAND trench A.10.c. Very little opposition in LE MESNIL. Many fires can be seen in the German back area. The heavy casualties are caused by the continued shelling & BERTHIOUTH trench & SNIPERS. A few snipers opposed us in LE MESNIL. Casualties. 2nd Coldstream Gds O.R. 5 killed 4 wounded 1 missing. 3rd — — — O.R. 2 wounded 1st Irish Gds O.R. 2 killed 11 wounded M.G. Coy O.R. 1 killed 2 wounded ———— ——— 8 — 19 — 1 — W.O. & discharged — 2nd Grenadiers Gds	
T.17.p.5.4.	18th		Cavalry reconnoitre LE MESNIL & HOLEQUISMY & MANANCOURT — Very little opposition to be encountered. The enemy appears to be covering their rearguard with a few snipers — Patrols pushed forward to HAYMAN COPSE & STAR X roads. W.O.C. & discharged — 2nd Grenadier Gds where 3rd Coldstream Gds like outposts line — Men booby traps encountered. Rum barrel of jam & trip wire on dugouts. Casualties — Canadian 3rd Coldstream Gds. Killed 1 wounded.	Appendix 342

Army Form C. 2118.

WAR DIARY
or
INTELLIGENCE SUMMARY

(Erase heading not required.)

Instructions regarding War Diaries and Intelligence Summaries are contained in F.S. Regs., Part II. and the Staff Manual respectively. Title Pages will be prepared in manuscript.

Place	Date	Hour	Summary of Events and Information	Remarks and references to Appendices
S.17.a.5.4 W.19.a.8.8	19th		Bde HQ. move to W.19.a.5.5. Cavalry reconnoitre LECHELLE - BUS - YTRES. A few snipers from in our flanks in MANCOURT & BARASTRE. Enemy seems to establish outpost in a general line W.12. central. 2nd Coldstream Gds believe 3rd Coldstream Gds W.5. central. 2nd Coldstream Gds in COULEAUX Gds in FREMICOURT - CORNET. Support 1st Bn Irish Gds Nore 2nd Coldstream Gds and mg's	A/M. 342
			Patrols sent out in search of outposts. Relief mentioned above takes place. Own Bn 2nd Coldstream Gds to relieve 3rd Gren. Gds on outpost line. Fins shortening to further within on the D Advanced system.	M/M. 344
W.19.a.8.8	20th			R/M. 345
			By means of each patrol that 60th Bde wd. take over Trench left with enemy. Notification received that 3rd Bde is to work in wave of railway Sécourcourt. On the 23rd inst. The Bde is to work in wave of railway on front in the Bde area - Own fn in rear of 2nd Coldstream Gds by whl. I not in the outpost line -	Aft. 346 R/M. 347
W.19.a.8.5	21st		METZ & 90 ROUNCOURT in fire.	

2449 Wt. W14957/M90 750,000 1/16 J.B.C. & A. Forms/C.2118/12.

WAR DIARY or INTELLIGENCE SUMMARY

Army Form C. 2118.

Instructions regarding War Diaries and Intelligence Summaries are contained in F. S. Regs., Part II. and the Staff Manual respectively. Title Pages will be prepared in manuscript.

(Erase heading not required.)

Place	Date	Hour	Summary of Events and Information	Remarks and references to Appendices
U.17.a.85.25	22		Situation unchanged. 2nd Bn. forward to Gromen T.19.a.55. Orders issued for occupation in man line of defence U.11.a.12. U.16.b.59. U.16.b.25. by 1 Coy of support troops. Orders issued for relief of the O.S.C. by 6th Bn. B.Dr. BEETROOT factory & t clerical recommences of found movement. Electrician gun to be in position	App 348 App 349 App 350
U.17.a.85.25	23rd		Man line of defence in U.11.a. Coloniam Sys. Field line wire. Relief of Hqs. Y 6th Bn. by 6/2 Bn of 1st Div. completed by 7 P.M. Battle Hqrs. to BOIS DOUAGE	
BOIS DOUAGE	24th		2 G.S. at Suzy. 2.C.G. at MAUREPAS. J.C.G. at MONTAUBAN. I.G. at COMBLES. Battn. began some improvement & construction of rows & railways to the forward area.	
BOIS DOUAGE	25th		G.O.C. with PERSONNE will major general	
BOIS DOUAGE	26th	S.Ph	Bad weather. Work of roads & railway continued. Conference at Bn HQ to discuss training & organisation. (5th C. Pamphlets SS 135/15 & 135/9/5)	

WAR DIARY
or
INTELLIGENCE SUMMARY

(Erase heading not required.)

Army Form C. 2118.

Place	Date	Hour	Summary of Events and Information	Remarks and references to Appendices
ARROW HEAD COPSE	27th		Brigade Headquarters moved during the day from BOIS DOUAGE (to ARROW HEAD COPSE, 750 yards East of the Southern end of TRONES WOOD.	
ARROW HEAD COPSE	28th		Bad weather and heavy rain. Work on 2 strong points and railways continued.	
ARROW HEAD COPSE	29th	12.0 noon	Brigadier attended a Conference at Divisional Head quarters. Training in general discussed.	
ARROW HEAD COPSE	30th	10.30 12.0 noon	Brigadier inspected billets of three Companies 3rd C.G. Brigadier had a Commanding Officers conference at Brigade Head quarters. Training discussed and questions arising from the trench held and Divisional Head quarters the previous day. Stiff wind and much rain and hail during day. In the after -noon Brigadier visited 2nd Bn C.G. working on LES BOEUFS - LE TRANSLOY road, 1st Gds Bde M.G. Coy working on GOMBLES-SAILLY road, 1st Bn C.G. and 1st I.G. working on LE TRANSLOY - LES BOEUFS road. Good work being done even when under very adverse conditions owing to the bad weather and lack of road metal.	

2.4.17.

J.A. Gifford
Brigadier General
Commanding 1st Guards Brigade

SECRET.   Copy No. 21

1st Guards Brigade Order No.104.

Ref.Maps - ALBERT 1/40,000.
       COMBLES 1/10,000.   March 9th, 1917.

1.   The 1st Guards Brigade will relieve 3rd Guards Brigade in the SAILLISEL Sector on the nights of March 12th/13th and 13th/14th in accordance with March Table attached.

2.   The Sector to be taken over extends from U.15.c.0.0. to U.8.central. Inter Bn. Boundary is at U.14.b.8.3.

3.   On completion of relief Battalions will be disposed as follows :-

    Right Battn.,   - H.Q. U.19.a.8.6.
                   3 Coy's. in front line and support.
                   1 Coy. BETTYS Reserve.

    Left Battn.,   - H.Q.,The HEBULE.
                   3 Coy's. in front line and support.
                   1 Coy. in HEBULE.

    Support Battn.,- H.Q., FREGICOURT.
                   2 Coy's.   "
                   1 Coy. HAIE WOOD.
                   1 Coy. COMBLES.

    Reserve Battn.,- MAUREPAS.

4.   Details of relief of Bde., Machine Gun Coy's. and Trench Mortar Bty's. will be arranged direct between Units concerned.

5.   Until completion of relief Units will come under Command of the G.O.C., Guards Brigade in whose area they are situated.

6.   Billeting parties of Battalions moving to FREGICOURT will report at FREGICOURT - HAIE Wood and COMBLES at 3 p.m. on the day on which their Units move to this Area.

    The Town Major COMBLES can point out the accommodation occupied by the Company in COMBLES.

    Billeting party of the Battalion moving to MAUREPAS will report at 9 a.m. on 14th inst., to Town Major MAUREPAS.

7.   1st Line Transport with the exception of Machine Gun Company and Brigade H.Q., Transport will remain in it's present position.

8.   Details of Battalions will be accommodated in the present Camps on application to the Camp Commandant concerned.

9.   Sapping Platoons of Battalions in the line will be accommodated at MOUCHOIR Copse, and until further Orders these Sapping Platoons will move in and out of the line with their Battalions.

(2)

10. Lorries are not available for the move. A Hut is set aside in MAUREPAS for the blankets of Battalions in the line and the Battalion at FREGICOURT.

11. The Foot Bath is in COMBLES *for the Support Bn.* near the old gum boot drying shed. The Battalion in Support will give notice to the N.C.O. in charge the evening before they intend to make use of it.

12. Each Battalion will detail 4 pack animals and 1 Limber complete turn-out to report to the Staff Captain at the Catacombs COMBLES at 3 p.m. on March 13th. These will be billeted in COMBLES under Brigade arrangements. They will be rationed by their Units.

13. Brigade H.Q., will close at BILLON and open at T.17.d.central at 3 p.m. on March 13th.

ACKNOWLEDGE.

Captain,
Brigade Major, 1st Guards Brigade.

Issued to Signals at 8 p.m.

```
Copy No.  1  2nd Bn. Grenadier Guards.
          2  2nd Bn. Coldstream Guards.
          3  3rd Bn. Coldstream Guards.
          4  1st Bn. Irish Guards.
          5  Bde., Machine Gun Company.
          6  1st Guards T. M. Battery.
          7  Guards Division.
          8  2nd Guards Brigade.
          9  3rd Guards Brigade.
         10  61st Infantry Brigade.
         11  Left Group, G.D.A.
         12  75th Field Coy., R.E.
         13  1st Gds. Bde. Supply Officer.
         14  1st Gds Bde. Transport Officer.
         15  Camp Commdt., BILLON.
         16     "       "   BRONFAY.
         17  Town Major, MAUREPAS.
         18     "     "   COMBLES.
         19  Staff Captain.
         20  O.C., Signals.
         20 - 25 Retained.
```

MARCH TABLE.

Date.	Unit.	From.	To.	Taking over from.	Remarks.
Mch.11th.	2/Cold.Gds.	BRONFAY.15.	FREGICOURT.	1/Gren.Gds.	(a) Leading troops not to enter COMBLES before 6 p.m. (b) 1 Offr. & 1 N.C.O. per Coy. & Bn.H.Q. to report at the HEBULE in the evening. Offrs. will go round the line. N.C.O's will remain and take over Stores etc.
	1st Gds.Bde. M.G.Coy. & T.M.Battery.	BILLON, Camp 16.	COMBLES Area.		(a) Accommodation will be allotted by Town Major COMBLES but accommodation is limited and Reserve teams must relieve Reserve teams direct. (b) To be clear of MAUREPAS by 5 p.m.
Mch.12th.	2/Cold.Gds.	FREGICOURT.	Left Sub-sector.	2/Scots Gds.	(a) No movement to take place before 7 pm. (b) Details as to guides etc. to be arranged direct. (c) 120 Tins of water & 250 prs of gum boots can be drawn at the end of the DECAUVILLE near the HEBULE. If these are not required 3 Gds.Bde. must be informed by 10 a.m.
	1/Irish Gds.	BILLON Camp 16.	FREGICOURT.	2/Cold.Gds.	(a) Leading troops not to enter COMBLES before 6-30 p.m. (b) 1 Offr. & 1 N.C.O. per Coy. & Bn.H.Q. to report at Bn.H.Q. U.19.a.8.8. during the evening. N.C.O's to remain in line & take over Stores etc. Offrs. to go round line and return.
	1st Gds.Bde. M.G.Coy. & T.M.Battery.	COMBLES Area.	Line.	3rd Gds.Bde. M.G.Coy. & T.M.Battery.	Relief not to start before 11 p.m.

Date.	Unit.	From.	To.	Taking over from.	Remarks.
ch.13th.	1/Irish Gds.		FREGICOURT.	Rt.Sub-sector. 4/Gren.Gds.	(a) No movement to take place before 7 p.m. (b) Details as to guides to be arranged direct. (c) Water & mns & Gum Boots can be drawn at the old store in GODBLES as required. Leading troops not to enter COMBLES before 6.30 p.m.
	3/Cold.Gds.	MILLON Camp 107.	FREGICOURT.	1/Irish Gds.	
	Brigade H.Q.	BILLON Wood.	T.17.d.5.5.	3/Gds.Bde.H.Q.	
ch.14th.	2/Gr.L.Gds.	BILLON Camp 107.	MAUREPAS.	4/Gren.Gds.	To start from Camp at 10 a.m.

All movement will be by Coys at 500 yards interval.

East of MAUREPAS all movement will be by platoons in file at 200 yds interval.

A gap of 200 yds will be kept between both 2 vehicles.

SECRET.

Amendment to 1st Guards Brigade Order No.104.

11th March 1917.

Reference 1st Guards Brigade Order No.104, the Transport and details of 2nd Bn. Grenadier Guards and 3rd Bn. Coldstream Guards will move to BROMBAY Camp 15 on March 14th and 15th respectively. Accommodation will be allotted by Camp Commandant BROMBAY 15.

Captain,

Brigade Major, 1st Guards Brigade.

Issued to :-

2nd Bn. Grenadier Guards.
3rd Bn. Coldstream Guards.
Guards Division.
Camp Commdt., Camp 15.
"   "   "   107.
Bde., Transport Officer.

SECRET.

1st Guards Brigade Warning Order No.105.

Ref. Map - COMBLES 1/10,000.   March 13th, 1917.

1. Indications show that enemy is likely to withdraw on our front in the near future.

2. If it is found at anytime that the enemy have evacuated their Front line, this will immediately be occupied by strong Patrols.
Such action must be reported at once to Brigade H.Q., and no further advance will take place until Orders are received from these H.Q.,

3. In the event of a further advance being Ordered, the first objective and the Brigade boundaries are shown on attached Map.

4. Two Coy's. from each Battalion in the Front line will push forward as Advanced Guard and establish Out-posts on the two spurs which run East from our line, i.e. :-

   (a) from U.10.c.8.0. to U.10.c.3.6.
   (b) U.4.c.0.0. to U.5.d.8.9. with a Post pushed forward to the N.E. corner of LOON COPSE.

5. When the objectives on these two spurs have been made good touch will be gained between Coy's. and with Brigades on the flanks.

6. One Advanced Guard Coy. from Left Battalion will be directed on the objective mentioned in 4 (b). This Coy. will be supported by the other Advanced Guard Coy. of Left Battalion.

   Similarly one Advanced Guard Coy. supported by the second Advanced Guard Coy. of Right Battalion will be directed on objective mentioned in 4 (a).

7. Coy's. must be distributed in depth.
   No attack on a large scale will be attempted but minor opposition must be dealt with by strong Patrols or by supporting Coy's. mentioned in 6.

8. The Coy. detailed to go forward will carry -

   2 bombs per man.
   4 sandbags.
   60% men shovels.
   25 flares per Company.

9. The objective when gained will be consolidated immediately.

   Troops in Reserve will be pushed up under cover of darkness to help in consolidation.

10. From Zero the Senior Comdg., Officer in the line will be in Command of the 4 Coy's. detailed to push forward as Advanced Guard and will establish his H.Q., at the present Coy. H.Q., in CANE ALLEY two hours before Zero.

    Each Battalion in the line will detail 2 Signallers to report at present H.Q., of above mentioned Officer.

    Bde., Signalling Officer will detail 1 Sgt. and 4 signallers. to this Officer at his H.Q., as soon as possible.

    A Battery Commander will be ordered to report at O.C., Advanced Guard H.Q., as early as possible. This Officer will deal with all Artillery support required by Advanced Guard Troops.

Each Advanced Guard Coy. will send 2 Runners to report at this Officers H.Q., as soon as possible.

11. From Zero all reports from Advanced Guard Coy's. will be sent to this Officer at CANE ALLEY.

As soon as Patrols report all clear, this Officer will move his H.Q., to about U.15.b.3.3.

The H.Q., in CANE ALLEY will be taken over by Brigade H.Q., as a transmitting Station.

12. In the event of an advance taking place, Brigade H.Q., will move to present Right Battalion H.Q., at U.19.a.6.3.

Battalion H.Q., of Battalions in the line will move to suitable positions about our present Support line.

13. As soon as it is reported that the enemy's Front line has been occupied by our Advanced Guard Coy's. – Orders will be issued to remaining two Coy's. of Battalions in the line to occupy our present Front and Support line but care must be taken to prevent overcrowding.

14. All ranks will be forbidden to enter any dug-out in the enemy line before it has been examined and passed safe by R.E.

15. Sections of R.E. will be pushed forward as soon as possible.

16. **Machine Guns and Stokes Mortars.**

Machine Guns will not move forward with Advanced Guard Troops, but O.C., Machine Gun Company will be prepared to push forward one Section after objectives have been gained.

Similarly the Trench Mortar Battery will be prepared to push forward a Section as ordered.

17. **Artillery.**

Batteries will be pushed forward as close as possible to SAILLISEL.

Captain,
Brigade Major, 1st Guards Brigade.

Copies to :-
    2nd Bn. Grenadier Guards.
    2nd Bn. Coldstream Guards.
    3rd Bn. Coldstream Guards.
    1st Bn. Irish Guards.
    Bde., Machine Gun Company.
    1st Guards T. M. Battery.

S E C R E T.　　　　　　　　　　　　　　　　1st G.B. No.1940/3.

2nd Bn. Grenadier Guards.　　　　2nd Guards Brigade.
2nd Bn. Coldstream Guards.　　　 61st Infantry Brigade.
3rd Bn. Coldstream Guards.　　　 Left Group, G.D.A.
1st Bn. Irish Guards.　　　　　　　75th Field Coy., R.E.
Bde., Machine Gun Company.　　 Bde., Signal Officer.
1st Guards T. M. Battery.　　　　Staff Captain.
Guards Division.

---

1. Herewith 1st Guards Brigade Provisional Defence Scheme.

2. This will come into force from 3 p.m. on March 13th.

3. Any alterations in dispositions must be reported at once to this Office.

4. Appendix "A", "Principles of Defence" has been issued and should be in possession of all Units of the 1st Guards Brigade. More Copies can be had on application to this Office.

5. Please acknowledge.

　　　　　　　　　　　　　　　　　　　　　Captain,
12th March 1917.　　　　　　　　Brigade Major, 1st Guards Brigade.

SECRET.   Copy No.......

            1ST GUARDS BRIGADE DEFENCE SCHEME. (PROVISIONAL).
                          SAILLISEL SECTOR.
  ----

1. BOUNDARIES.

    (a) The SAILLISEL Sector extends from U.15.c.0.0. to U.8.b.2.2.
    (b) Inter-battalion boundary is at U.14.b.6.8.
    (c) Brigade boundaries are shown on the attached map.
    (d) The 2nd Guards Brigade is on our right and the 61st Infantry
        Brigade on our left.

2. ORGANISATION OF DEFENCE.

    (a) Front Line.
        From U.15.c.0.0. - U.14.b.4.8. the front line is a series of
        posts, except for GREEN HOWARD (U.14.d.10.3. - U.14.b.9.2.)
        From U.14.b.4.8. a continuous SWITCH TRENCH runs to POTSDAM
        TRENCH, which is itself continuous as far as U.8.d.1.8.
        In front of POTSDAM is a "T" head, consisting of a short
        communication trench and about 150 yards of PALZ TRENCH.

    (b) Support Line.
        BETTYE RESERVE (about U.14.c.8.0. - 6.3.)
        A series of posts, 9 - 1 (about U.14.d.6.7. - b.5.3.)
        CANE ALLEY (U.14.b.1.3. - 3.7. - 0.8.)
        CHEESE SUPPORT (U.8.c.7½.5. - 8.10.)

    (c) Reserve Line.
        A semi-circle of posts round East side of BULLET CROSS ROADS
        (U.20.a.4½.9½.)
        BULL DOG RESERVE, (in posts) for 50 yards South of the
        FREGICOURT ROAD and 200 yards North of it.
        SOUTH COPSE Strong Point, U.13.a.8.3.
        COPSE RESERVE (in posts, not yet begun.)

    (d) Intermediate Line.
        Through T.24.central and T.18.central. Wired throughout
        and dug in a few places.

    (e) Switch Line.
        Portion of BISHOPS AVENUE SWITCH, in T.24.d.   Wired but
        not dug.

    (f) Second Line.
        Just outside Eastern outskirts of COMBLES, and including
        Cemetery Strong Point.   Wired, but, with the exception of
        the Strong Point, not dug.

3. DISTRIBUTION.

            Brigade Headquarters   -   T.17.d.8.3.

            Right Front Battalion.   U
            Battalion Headquarters   -   .19.a.8.7.
            1 Company   -   Posts 10 - 17.
            1 Company   -   GREEN HOWARD.
            1 Company   -   Support Posts 9 - 1, and CANE ALLEY
            1 Company   -   BETTYE RESERVE & BULL DOG.

                                  1.

Left Front Battalion.
Battalion Headquarters — HEBULE, U.13.a.3.5.
1 Company — PALZ & POTSDAM Right.
1 Company — POTSDAM Left & HEBULE.
1 Company — Right Support (about U.14.b.5.7.) & CHEESE SUPPORT.
1 Company — HEBULE, U.13.a.3.5. with 1 Platoon garrisoning SOUTH COPSE Strong Point.

Support Battalion.
Battalion Headquarters — FREGICOURT.
1 Company — FREGICOURT.
2 Companies — HAIE WOOD.
1 Company — COMBLES.

Reserve Battalion. — MAUREPAS.

Brigade M. G. Company.
Headquarters — HAIE WOOD.
For position of Guns see Appendix "B".

Brigade T. M. Battery.
Headquarters — COMBLES (temporary).
For position of Guns see Appendix "C".

55th Field Company R.E. — COMBLES CATACOMBS.

4. TACTICAL FEATURES.

Our hold on the ridge East of the BAPAUME ROAD denies the enemy observation of the COMBLES VALLEY. Should the enemy obtain this observation the whole of our position East of COMBLES will become a very costly one to hold.

If the Front System on the Right Battalion Sub-sector is lost, the enemy will still be denied full observation as long as the high ground round BULLET CROSS ROADS is held.

The Valley running East and West just South of SAILLY SAILLISEL, can best be defended by cross fire from the high ground on each side of it.

5. ARTILLERY.

The Brigade is supported by Left Group, Guards Divnl. Artillery.
H.Q., Left Group — COMBLES.
Each Battalion in the Line is in direct communication with a Battery. These communications must be frequently tested.

Counter preparation will be ordered by the Corps or Division in case of information being received of a hostile bombardment of such a nature as to indicate a probable hostile attack.

6. ACTION IN THE EVENT OF ATTACK.

(a) In the event of the enemy gaining a footing in any part of our line, the troops on both flanks will hold their ground and will on no account give way. Lewis Gun and Rifle Grenade fire will immediately be brought to bear from the flanks on that portion of the line occupied by the enemy. A good supply of Rifle Grenades should therefore be kept in the line. Should this fail to turn the enemy out an immediate counter attack from the Support Line Posts where such exist will be delivered under cover of Rifle Grenade, Lewis Gun and Trench Mortar barrage

The Right Battalion in the line may draw to the extent of 2 of 2 Platoons, and Left Battalion to the extent of 3 Platoons from it's Reserve Coy's. for the purpose of reinforcing it's Support line with a view to such counter-attacks, but the remainder of the garrison of the Reserve line and the garrison of SOUTH COPSE Strong Point will hold it's ground at all costs and will not be used in any counter-attack.

(b) Commdg., Officers and Company Commdrs., must reconnoitre as soon as possible the ground routes and trenches West of the SAILLY SAILLISEL - PERONNE Road in the Brigade Area.

The position of the following deep dug-outs should also be known :-

T.18.d.3.1½. - T.18.d.1.4. - U.14.a.0.4. - U.14.c. 2.8.

(c) On receipt of message "Defence Scheme prepare to move", Support and Reserve Coy's. Battn's. will be prepared to move at a moments notice.
The O.C., Reserve Battn., will report at Brigade H.Q., as soon as possible.
The O.C., Support Battn., will send an Officer to report at Brigade H.Q., as soon as possible.
Battalions will draw 2 bombs - 4 sandbags per man and 100 flares per Battalion from the nearest Store.
Troops of these Battalions if ordered to move will parade in Fighting Order - water bottles will be filled and if possible, one days ration in addition to the Iron Ration carried.

(d) The Machine Guns in Brigade Reserve will be prepared to move either to the Intermediate Line or into the Reserve Line. The most suitable extra positions in these Lines will be reconnoitred by O.C., and Section Commdrs., of Brigade Machine Gun Company.

(e) The Reserve Sections of the Trench Mortar Battery will be prepared to move as ordered. All Officers of the Battery must reconnoitre the Reserve Line and the best way to it.
Guns in the Line must be in the closest touch with the O.C., Company in whose Area they are situated.
New offensive emplacements for all Guns of the Battery must be constructed as soon as possible.

(f) The 75th Field Coy., R.E. (H.Q., COMBLES Catacombs) will "Stand To" in billets and await order.

(g) All fatigue and carrying parties will report at once to the nearest H.Q.,

7. GAS.

Box respirators will be worn by all ranks East of MAUREPAS. In the event of a Gas Attack or Gas Shelling, Units will act in accordance with 4th Army Standing Orders for Defence against Gas.

8. WIRELESS.

There is a Wireless Set at SAILLY Church, the position of which must be known to all Runners of Front and Support Coy's.

9. "S.O.S".

The "S.O.S" telephone or rocket signal means that the enemy are actually leaving their trenches and that Rapid Barrage is required from Artillery and Machine Guns that can barrage in front of our Front Line.

The XIV Corps "S.O.S" rocket is at present - 1 Green, 1 White, 1 Green, fired in quick succession and repeated until acted upon.

Captain,

12th March 1917.

Brigade Major, 1st Guards Brigade.

APPENDIX "B".

DISPOSITION ON MACHINE GUNS.

Disposition.	No. of Gun.	Map reference.
Front Line	N.5.	U.14.a.3.8½.
	U.5.	U.8.d.2.8.
Support Line	O.2.	U.14.c.9.2½.
	N.3.	U.14.d.3½.8.
	N.4.	U.14.b.3½.3.
	P.3.	U.14.a.7.4.
	U.1.	U.14.a.9.6½.
	U.4.	U.8.c.8.9.
Reserve Line	P.2.	U.14.c.2.3.
	Q.4.	U.13.a.7.2.
	W.1.	U.13.b.5.5.
	W.2.	U.7.d.7.7.
Intermediate Line	Q.3.	T.18.d.2.8.
	X.2.	T.13.a.8.2.
Reserve Guns	-	HAIE WOOD.

APPENDIX "C".

DISPOSITION OF LIGHT TRENCH MORTARS.

U.14.b.3.5.   )   Fire on road and trench junction
U.14.b.3.6.   )   about U.14.b.9.8.

APPENDIX "D".

MEDICAL ARRANGEMENTS.

(a) Normal conditions.

Battalion Aid Posts will be cleared by Battalion Stretcher Bearers to the Bearer Posts at T.24.b.9.1 and at the HEBULE respectively.
The Bearer Post at T.24.b.0.1 will be cleared by Ambulance Cars to A.D.S. at T.28.d.8.9
The Bearer Post at HEBULE will be cleared to HAIE WOOD Bearer Post by Field Ambulance Bearers and thence by Ambulance Cars or Decauville to CATACOMBS, COMBLES.
The A.D.S. at T.28.d.8.9 and at CATACOMBS will be cleared by Ambulance Cars to TRONES WOOD Dressing Station (XIV Corps) and thence by Motor Ambulance Convoy Cars to Casualty Clearing Station, GROVETOWN.

(b) In the event of Hostile Attack.

Bearer Post will be reinforced by No. 4 Field Ambulance, and Bearer Squads pushed forward to assist Battalion Stretcher Bearers to clear Battalion Aid Posts.
Horse Ambulance will reinforce Ambulance Cars at T.24.b.9.1. and HAIE WOOD.

APPENDIX "E".

BRIGADE BOMB STORES.

FREGICOURT (Right Battalion)	-	T.24.b.9.1.
HEBULE (Left Battalion)	-	U.13.a.3.5.
HAIE WOOD (Left Battalion)	-	T.23.b.9.5. (Subsidiary Dump).
COMBLES (Rear Dump)	-	T.28.b.1.1.

R.E. DUMPS.

AID POST	-	U.19.a.8.6.
HAIE WOOD	-	T.23.b.9.5.

SALVAGE DUMPS.

Right Battalion	-	U.19.a.7.5.
Left Battalion	-	HEBULE. U.13.a.3.5.

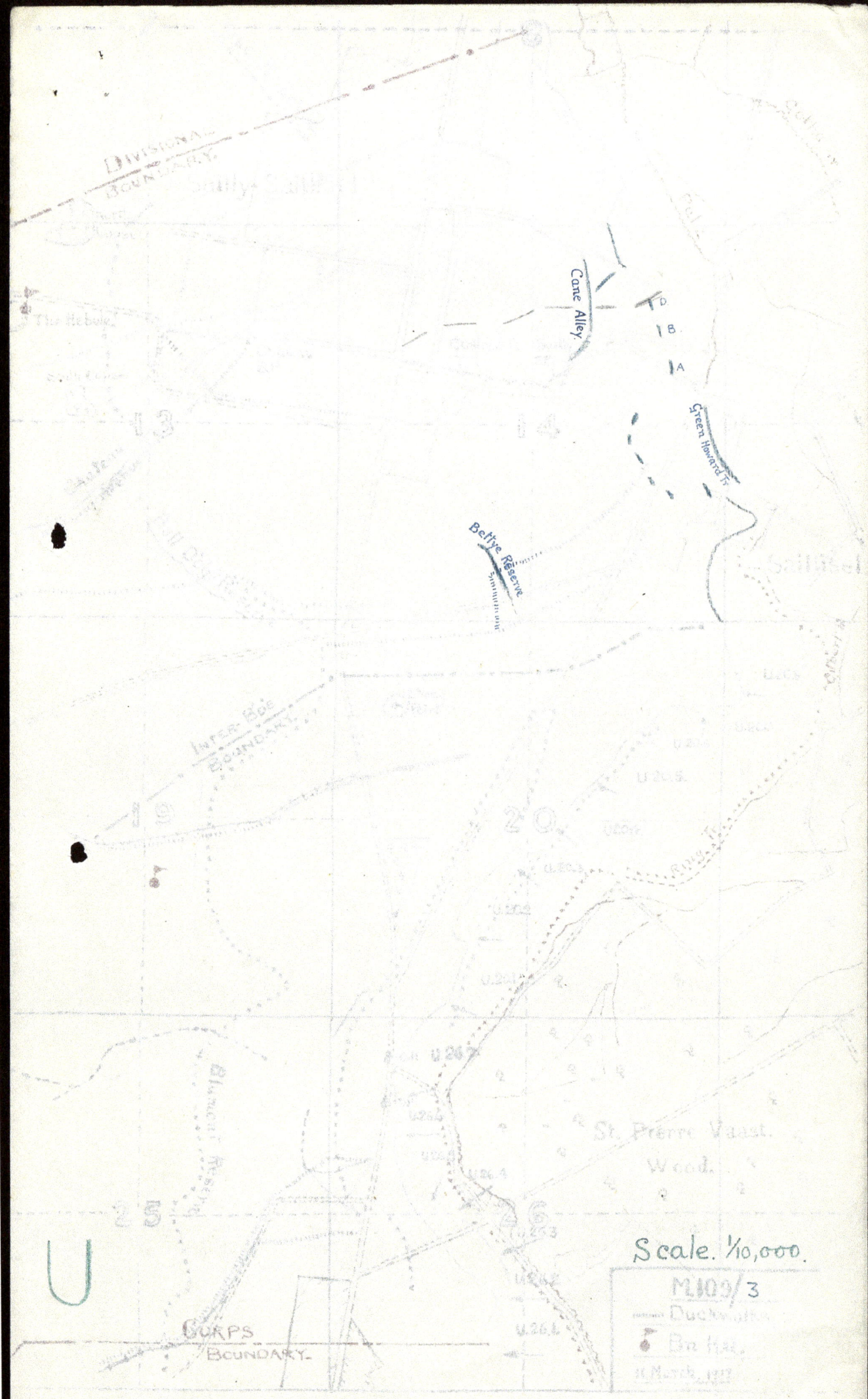

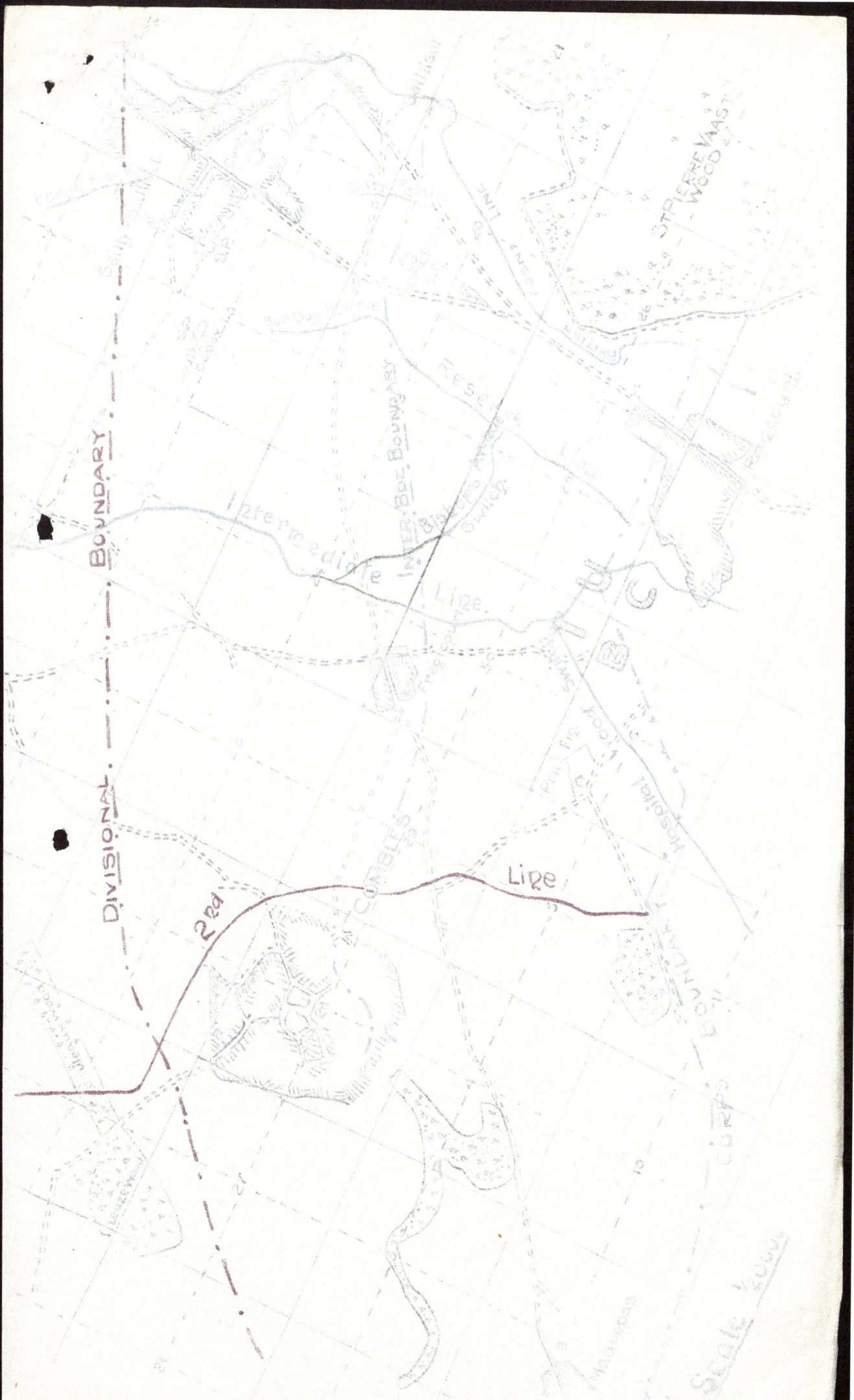

SECRET.   Copy No. 23

1st Guards Brigade Order No.104.

Ref. Maps - ALBERT 1/40,000.   March 9th, 1917.
         COMBLES 1/10,000.

1.   The 1st Guards Brigade will relieve 3rd Guards Brigade in the SAILLISEL Sector on the nights of March 12th/13th and 13th/14th in accordance with March Table attached.

2.   The Sector to be taken over extends from U.15.c.0.0. to U.8.central. Inter Bn. Boundary is at U.14.b.6.3.

3.   On completion of relief Battalions will be disposed as follows :-

    Right Battn., - H.Q. U.19.a.3.6.
                  3 Coy's. in front line and support.
                  1 Coy. BETTYS Reserve.

    Left Battn.,   - H.Q., The HEBULE.
                  3 Coy's. in front line and support.
                  1 Coy. in HEBULE.

    Support Battn.,- H.Q., FREGICOURT.
                    2 Coy's. "
                  1 Coy. HAIE WOOD.
                  1 Coy. COMBLES.

    Reserve Battn.,- MAUREPAS.

4.   Details of relief of Bde., Machine Gun Coy's. and Trench Mortar Bty's. will be arranged direct between Units concerned.

5.   Until completion of relief Units will come under Command of the G.O.C., Guards Brigade in whose area they are situated.

6.   Billeting parties of Battalions moving to FREGICOURT will report at FREGICOURT - HAIE Wood and COMBLES at 3 p.m. on the day on which their Units move to this Area.

      The Town Major COMBLES can point out the accommodation occupied by the Company in COMBLES.

      Billeting party of the Battalion moving to MAUREPAS will report at 9 a.m. on 14th inst., to Town Major MAUREPAS.

7.   1st Line Transport with the exception of Machine Gun Company and Brigade H.Q., Transport will remain in it's present position.

8.   Details of Battalions will be accommodated in the present Camps on application to the Camp Commandant concerned.

9.   Sapping Platoons of Battalions in the line will be accommodated at MOUCHOIR Copse, and until further Orders these Sapping Platoons will move in and out of the line with their Battalions.

(2)

10. Lorries are not available for the move. A Hut is set aside in MAUREPAS for the blankets of Battalions in the line and the Battalion at FREGICOURT.

11. The Foot Bath is in COMBLES near the old gum boot drying shed. The Battalion in Support will give notice to the N.C.O. in charge the evening before they intend to make use of it.
for the Support Bn.

12. Each Battalion will detail 4 pack animals and 1 Limber complete turn-out to report to the Staff Captain at the Catacombs COMBLES at 3 p.m. on March 13th. These will be billeted in COMBLES under Brigade arrangements. They will be rationed by their Units.

13. Brigade H.Q., will close at BILLON and open at T.17.d.central at 3 p.m. on March 13th.

    ACKNOWLEDGE.

                                                          Captain,
                            Brigade Major, 1st Guards Brigade.

Issued to Signals at 8 p.m.

       Copy No. 1 2nd Bn. Grenadier Guards.
               2 2nd Bn. Coldstream Guards.
               3 3rd Bn. Coldstream Guards.
               4 1st Bn. Irish Guards.
               5 Bde., Machine Gun Company.
               6 1st Guards T. M. Battery.
               7 Guards Division.
               8 2nd Guards Brigade.
               9 3rd Guards Brigade.
              10 61st Infantry Brigade.
              11 Left Group, G.D.A.
              12 75th Field Coy., R.E.
              13 1st Gds.Bde. Supply Officer.
              14 1st Gds.Bde. Transport Officer.
              15 Camp Commdt., BILLON.
              16 "   " BRONFAY.
              17 Town Major, MAUREPAS.
              18 "   " COMBLES.
              19 Staff Captain.
              20 O.C., Signals.
              20 - 25 Retained.

MARCH TABLE.

Date.	Unit.	From.	To.	Taking over from.	Remarks.
Mch.11th.	2/Cold.Gds.	BRONFAY.15.	FREGICOURT.	1/Gren.Gds.	(a) Leading troops not to enter COMBLES before 6 p.m. (b) 1 Offr.& 1 N.C.O. per Coy. & Bn.H.Q. to report at the HEBULE in the evening. Offrs. will go round the line. N.C.O's will remain and take over Stores etc.
	1st Gds.Bde. H.Q.Coy. & T.M.Battery.	BILLON,Camp 16.	COMBLES Area.		(a) Accommodation will be allotted by Town Major COMBLES but accommodation is limited and Reserve teams must relieve Reserve teams direct. (b) To be clear of MAUREPAS by 5 p.m. (c) No movement to take place before 7 p.m. (b) Details as to guides etc. to be arranged direct. (c) 120 Tins of water & 250 prs of gum boots can be drawn at the end of the DECAUVILLE near the HEBULE. If these are not required 3 Gds.Bde. must be informed by 10 a.m.
Mch.12th.	2/Cold.Gds.	FREGICOURT.	Left Sub-sector.	2/Scots Gds.	
	1/Irish Gds.	BILLON Camp 16.FREGICOURT.		2/Cold.Gds.	(a) Leading troops not to enter COMBLES before 6.30 p.m. (b) 1 Offr.& 1 N.C.O. per Coy. & Bn.H.Q. to report at Bn.H.Q. U.19.a.8.6. during the evening. N.C.O's to remain in line & take over Stores etc. Offrs. to go round line and return.
	1st Gds.Bde. H.Q.Coy. & T.M.Battery.	COMBLES Area.	Line.	3rd Gds.Bde. H.Q.Coy. & T.M.Battery.	Relief not to start before 11 p.m.

Date.	Unit.	From.	To.	Taking over from.	Remarks.
ch.13th.	1/Irish Gds.	FREGICOURT.	Rt.Sub-sector.	4/Gren.Gds.	(a) No movement to take place before 7 p.m. (b) Details as to guides to be arranged direct. (c) Water & Wire & Gum Boots can be drawn at the old store in COMBLES as required.
	3/Cold.Gds.	BILLON Camp 107.	FREGICOURT.	1/Irish Gds.	Leading troops not to enter COMBLES before 6 p.m.
	Brigade H.Q.,	BILLON Wood.	T.17.d.5.5.	3/Gds.Bde.H.Q.,	
ch.14th.	2/Gren.Gds.	BILLON Camp 107.	MAUREPAS.	4/Gren.Gds.	To start from Camp at 10 a.m.

All movement will be by Coy's. in file at 500 yards interval.

East of MAUREPAS all movement will be by Platoons in file at 200 yards interval.

A gap of 200 yards will be left between every 2 vehicles.

SECRET.   1st G.B. No.1940/3.

2nd Bn. Grenadier Guards.	2nd Guards Brigade.
2nd Bn. Coldstream Guards.	61st Infantry Brigade.
3rd Bn. Coldstream Guards.	Loft Group, G.D.A.
1st Bn. Irish Guards.	75th Field Coy., R.E.
Bde., Machine Gun Company.	Bde., Signal Officer.
1st Guards T. M. Battery.	Staff Captain.
Guards Division.	

1. Herewith 1st Guards Brigade Provisional Defence Scheme.

2. This will come into force from 3 p.m. on March 13th.

3. Any alterations in dispositions must be reported at once to this Office.

4. Appendix "A", "Principles of Defence" has been issued and should be in possession of all Units of the 1st Guards Brigade. More Copies can be had on application to this Office.

5. Please acknowledge.

                                                    Captain,
12th March 1917.   Brigade Major, 1st Guards Brigade.

S E C R E T.   Copy No.......

1ST GUARDS BRIGADE DEFENCE SCHEME. (PROVISIONAL).
SAILLISEL SECTOR.

1. **BOUNDARIES.**

    (a) The SAILLISEL Sector extends from U.15.c.0.0. to U.8.b.2.2.
    (b) Inter-battalion boundary is at U.14.b.6.6.
    (c) Brigade boundaries are shown on the attached map.
    (d) The 2nd Guards Brigade is on our right and the 61st Infantry Brigade on our left.

2. **ORGANISATION OD DEFENCE.**

    (a) Front Line.
    From U.15.c.0.0. - U.14.b.4.8. the front line is a series of posts, except for GREEN HOWARD (U.14.d.10.3. - U.14.b.9.2.)
    From U.14.b.4.8. a continuous SWITCH TRENCH runs to POTSDAM TRENCH, which is itself continuous as far as U.8.d.1.8.
    In front of POTSDAM is a "T" head, consisting of a short communication trench and about 150 yards of PALZ TRENCH.

    (b) Support Line.
    BETTYE RESERVE (about U.14.c.8.0. - 6.3.)
    A series of posts, 9 - 1 (about U.14.d.6.7. - b.5.3.)
    CANE ALLEY (U.14.b.1.3. - 3.7. - 0.8.)
    CHEESE SUPPORT (U.8.c.7½.5. - 8.10.)

    (c) Reserve Line.
    A semi-circle of posts round East side of BULLET CROSS ROADS (U.20.a.½.9½.)
    BULL DOG RESERVE, (in posts) for 50 yards South of the FREGICOURT ROAD and 200 yards North of it.
    SOUTH COPSE Strong Point, U.13.a.8.3.
    COPSE RESERVE (in posts, not yet begun.)

    (d) Intermediate Line.
    Through T.24.central and T.18.central. Wired throughout and dug in a few places.

    (e) Switch Line.
    Portion of BISHOPS AVENUE SWITCH, in T.24.d. Wired but not dug.

    (f) Second Line.
    Just outside Eastern outskirts of COMBLES, and including Cemetery Strong Point. Wired, but, with the exception of the Strong Point, not dug.

3. **DISTRIBUTION.**

    Brigade Headquarters   -   T.17.d.8.3.

    Right Front Battalion.
    Battalion Headquarters   -   U.19.a.8.7.
    1 Company   -   Posts 10 - 17.
    1 Company   -   GREEN HOWARD.
    1 Company   -   Support Posts 9 - 1, and CANE ALLEY
    1 Company   -   BETTYE RESERVE & BULL DOG.

1.

-2-

Left Front Battalion.
Battalion Headquarters — HEBULE, U.13.a.3.5.
1 Company   — PALZ & POTSDAM Right.
1 Company   — POTSDAM Left & HEBULE.
1 Company   — Right Support (about U.14.b.5.7.) & CHEESE SUPPORT.
1 Company   — HEBULE, U.13.a.3.5. with 1 Platoon garrisoning SOUTH COPSE Strong Point.

Support Battalion.
Battalion Headquarters — FREGICOURT.
1 Company   — FREGICOURT.
2 Companies   — HAIE WOOD.
1 Company   — COMBLES.

Reserve Battalion.   — MAUREPAS.

Brigade M. G. Company.
Headquarters   — HAIE WOOD.
For position of Guns see Appendix "B".

Brigade T. M. Battery.
Headquarters   — COMBLES (temporary).
For position of Guns see Appendix "C".

55th Field Company R.E. — COMBLES CATACOMBS.

4. TACTICAL FEATURES.

Our hold on the ridge East of the BAPAUME ROAD denies the enemy observation of the COMBLES VALLEY. Should the enemy obtain this observation the whole of our position East of COMBLES will become a very costly one to hold.

If the Front System on the Right Battalion Sub-sector is lost, the enemy will still be denied full observation as long as the high ground round BULLET CROSS ROADS is held.

The Valley running East and West just South of SAILLY SAILLISEL, can best be defended by cross fire from the high ground on each side of it.

5. ARTILLERY.

The Brigade is supported by Left Group, Guards Divnl. Artillery.
H.Q., Left Group — COMBLES.
Each Battalion in the Line is in direct communication with a Battery. These communications must be frequently tested.

Counter preparation will be ordered by the Corps or Division in case of information being received of a hostile bombardment of such a nature as to indicate a probable hostile attack.

6. ACTION IN THE EVENT OF ATTACK.

(a) In the event of the enemy gaining a footing in any part of our line, the troops on both flanks will hold their ground and will on no account give way. Lewis Gun and Rifle Grenade fire will immediately be brought to bear from the flanks on that portion of the line occupied by the enemy. A good supply of Rifle Grenades should therefore be kept in the line. Should this fail to turn the enemy out an immediate counter attack from the Support Line Posts where such exist will be delivered under cover of Rifle Grenade, Lewis Gun and Trench Mortar barrage

- 3 -

The Right Battalion in the line may draw to the extent of 2 of 2 Platoons, and Left Battalion to the extent of 3 Platoons from it's Reserve Coy's. for the purpose of reinforcing it's Support line with a view to such counter-attacks, but the remainder of the garrison of the Reserve line and the garrison of SOUTH COPSE Strong Point will hold it's ground at all costs and will not be used in any counter-attack.

(b)   Commdg., Officers and Company Commdrs., must reconnoitre as soon as possible the ground routes and trenches West of the SAILLY SAILLISEL - PERONNE Road in the Brigade Area.

The position of the following deep dug-outs should also be known :-
T.18.d.3.1½. - T.18.d.1.4. - U.14.a.0.4. - U.14.c. 2.8.

(c)   On receipt of message "Defence Scheme prepare to move", Support and Reserve Coy's. Battn's. will be prepared to move at a moments notice.
The O.C., Reserve Battn., will report at Brigade H.Q., as soon as possible.
The O.C., Support Battn., will send an Officer to report at Brigade H.Q., as soon as possible.
Battalions will draw 2 bombs - 4 sandbags per man and 100 flares per Battalion from the nearest Store.
Troops of these Battalions if ordered to move will parade in Fighting Order - water bottles will be filled and if possible, one days ration in addition to the Iron Ration carried.

(d)   The Machine Guns in Brigade Reserve will be prepared to move either to the Intermediate Line or into the Reserve Line. The most suitable extra positions in these Lines will be reconnoitred by O.C., and Section Commdrs., of Brigade Machine Gun Company.

(e)   The Reserve Sections of the Trench Mortar Battery will be prepared to move as ordered. All Officers of the Battery must reconnoitre the Reserve Line and the best way to it.
Guns in the Line must be in the closest touch with the O.C., Company in whose Area they are situated.
New offensive emplacements for all Guns of the Battery must be constructed as soon as possible.

(f)   The 75th Field Coy., R.E. (H.Q., COMBLES Catacombs) will "Stand To" in billets and await order.

(g)   All fatigue and carrying parties will report at once to the nearest H.Q.,

7. GAS.

Box respirators will be worn by all ranks East of MAUREPAS. In the event of a Gas Attack or Gas Shelling, Units will act in accordance with 4th Army Standing Orders for Defence against Gas.

8. WIRELESS.

There is a Wireless Set at SAILLY Church, the position of which must be known to all Runners of Front and Support Coy's.

9. **"S.O.S".**

The "S.O.S" telephone or rocket signal means that the enemy are actually leaving their trenches and that Rapid Barrage is required from Artillery and Machine Guns that can barrage in front of our Front Line.

The XIV Corps "S.O.S" rocket is at present - 1 Green, 1 White, 1 Green, fired in quick succession and repeated until acted upon.

Captain,

12th March 1917.   Brigade Major, 1st Guards Brigade.

APPENDIX "B".

DISPOSITION ON MACHINE GUNS.

Disposition.	No. of Gun.	Map reference.
Front Line	N.5.	U.14.a.3.8½.
	U.5.	U.8.d.2.8.
Support Line	O.2.	U.14.c.9.2½.
	N.3.	U.14.d.3½.8.
	N.4.	U.14.b.3½.3.
	P.3.	U.14.a.7.4.
	U.1.	U.14.a.9.6½.
	U.4.	U.8.c.8.9.
Reserve Line	P.2.	U.14.c.2.3.
	Q.4.	U.13.a.7.2.
	W.1.	U.13.b.5.5.
	W.2.	U.7.d.7.7.
Intermediate Line	Q.3.	T.18.d.2.8.
	X.2.	T.18.a.8.2.
Reserve Guns	–	MAIE WOOD.

APPENDIX "C".

DISPOSITION OF LIGHT TRENCH MORTARS.

U.14.b.3.5.) Fire on road and trench junction
U.14.b.3.6.) about U.14.b.9.8.

APPENDIX "D".

MEDICAL ARRANGEMENTS.

(a) **Normal conditions.**

Battalion Aid Posts will be cleared by Battalion Stretcher Bearers to the Bearer Posts at T.24.b.9.1 and at the HEBULE respectively.
The Bearer Post at T.24.b.0.1 will be cleared by Ambulance Cars to A.D.S. at T.28.d.8.9.
The Bearer Post at HEBULE will be cleared to HAIE WOOD Bearer Post by Field Ambulance Bearers and thence by Ambulance Cars or Decauville to CATACOMBS, COMBLES.
The A.D.S. at T.28.d.8.9. and at CATACOMBS will be cleared by Ambulance Cars to TRONES WOOD Dressing Station (XIV Corps) and thence by Motor Ambulance Convoy Cars to Casualty Clearing Station, GROVETOWN.

(b) **In the event of Hostile Attack.**

Bearer Post will be reinforced by No. 4 Field Ambulance, and Bearer Squads pushed forward to assist Battalion Stretcher Bearers to clear Battalion Aid Posts.
Horse Ambulance will reinforce Ambulance Cars at T.24.b.9.1. and HAIE WOOD.

APPENDIX "E".

BRIGADE BOMB STORES.

FREGICOURT (Right Battalion)	-	T.24.b.9.1.
HEBULE (Left Battalion)	-	U.13.a.3.5.
HAIE WOOD (Left Battalion)	-	T.23.b.9.5. (Subsidiary Dump).
COMBLES (Rear Dump)	-	T.28.b.1.1.

R.E. DUMPS.

AID POST	-	U.19.a.8.6.
HAIE WOOD	-	T.23.b.9.5.

SALVAGE DUMPS.

Right Battalion	-	U.19.a.7.5.
Left Battalion	-	HEBULE. U.13.a.3.5.

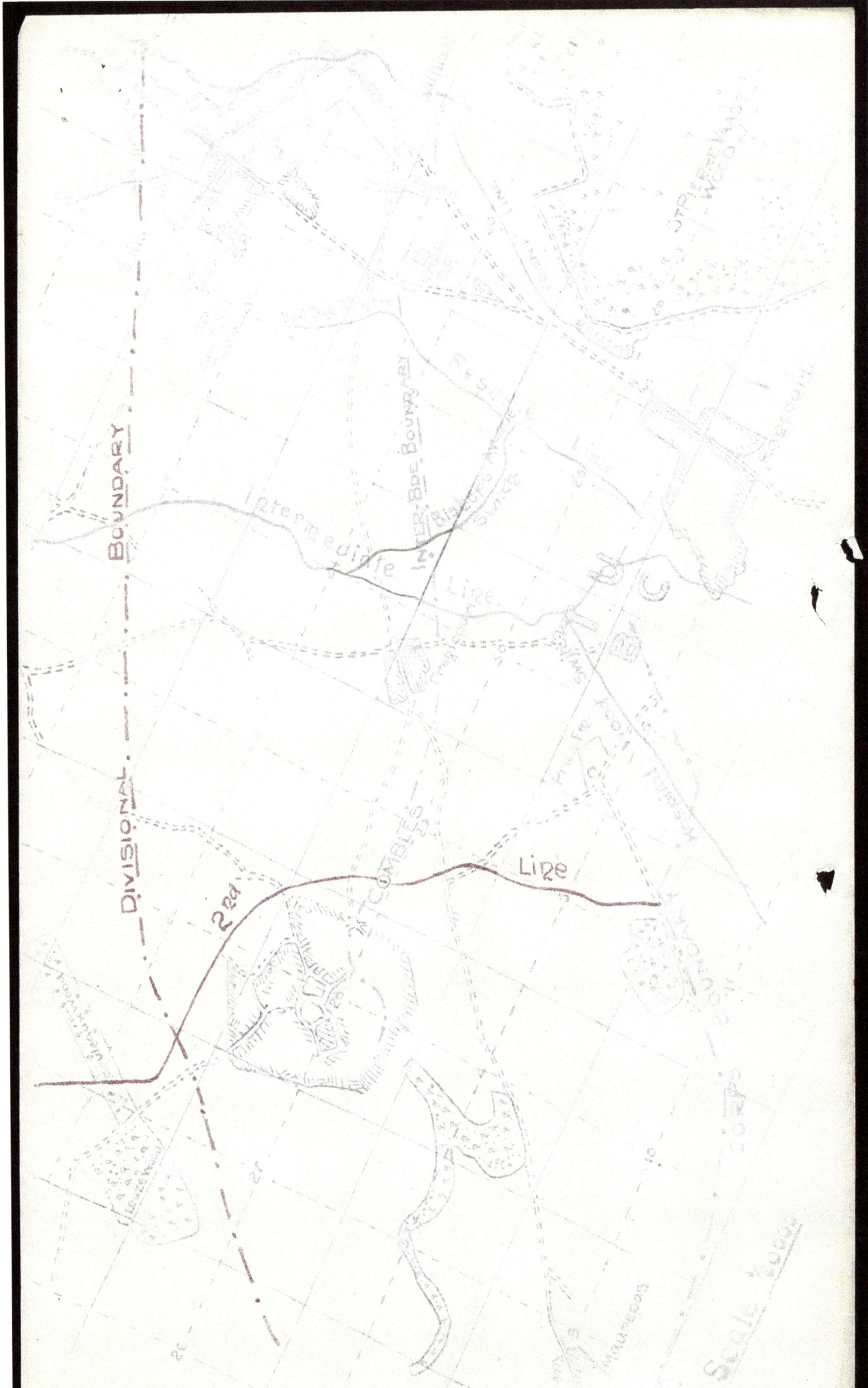

1st Guards Brigade Intelligence Report.

8 a.m. Mch. 13th to 8 a.m. Mch. 14th.

OPERATIONS.

Very little rifle or Machine Gun fire. We fired a few Rifle Grenades in retaliation for German Rifle Grenades.

INTELLIGENCE.

Work in progress was noticed at U 3 c 4.5. A dugout and an O.P. are suspected here.

Various other small parties of Germans were seen at different times at U 8 d 7.2, and in the vicinity of ROCQUIGNY.

A very large number of Very Lights were put up from the German Front and Support Lines. Green lights were apparently sent up as a Signal for the Artillery to lengthen range and Green and Red for the Artillery to cease fire.

Our wire in front of No. 1, 2, 3, 4 & 5 Posts was observed to be very weak. It consists of a continuous row of French wire without any barbed wire.

AIRCRAFT.

At about 6 p.m. 5 small German Tractor Biplanes were flying at an altitude of from 2000 to 3000 ft. over SAILLY SAILLISEL. They remained in the vicinity for half-an-hour and were fired upon by Machine Guns from the ground without effect.

ARTILLERY.

The area chiefly shelled was SAILLY WOOD. There was a good deal of indiscriminate shelling over the remainder of the Brigade Sector.

MACHINE GUNS.

Hostile Machine Guns fired short bursts with intervals of about an hour throughout the night down the main SAILLY - BAPAUME Road.

Captain,
for Brigade Major, 1st Guards Brigade.

SECRET.   1st G.B. No.117.

Bde., Machine Gun Company.
Bde., Trench Mortar Battery.
2nd Bn. Grenadier Guards.
2nd Bn. Coldstream Guards.   ) (for information.)
3rd Bn. Coldstream Guards.
1st Bn. Irish Guards.

1.   1st Guards Brigade Machine Gun Company and Trench
Mortar Battery will move tomorrow 27th inst., to LE
TRANSLOY Area - G.26.a. - where they will be camped.

2.   The Machine Gun Company and Trench Mortar Battery
will not pass E. of the BEAULENCOURT - CAILLY SAILLISEL
Road before 5 p.m.

3.   Billeting parties will report to a representative of
"Q" Branch, Guards Division, at N.30.b.8.5. at 12 noon.

4.   Machine Guns and Trench Mortars will be stored at
MAUREPAS Camp and will be under the charge of the details
left behind.   O.C., Bde. Machine Gun Company and O.C., Bde.
Trench Mortar Battery will communicate direct with Camp
Commandant, MAUREPAS, concerning this.

5.   The C.R.E. Guards Division will issue instructions
for work on the SOUTH COPSE Decauville Railway which will
begin on March 28th.

6.   Administrative Orders G.D. No.797/40/A are attached.

ACKNOWLEDGE.

                                                        Captain.
26th March 1917.   Brigade Major, 1st Guards Brigade.

S E C R E T.   33)/A   1st G.B. No.1940.

2nd Bn. Grenadier Guards.   2nd Guards Brigade.
2nd Bn. Coldstream Guards.   21st Infantry Brigade.
3rd Bn. Coldstream Guards.   75th Field Coy., R.E.
1st Bn. Irish Guards.   Left Group, G.D.A.
Bde., Machine Gun Company.   1st Gds. Bde. Supply Officer.
1st Guards T. M. Battery.   1st Gds. Bde. Transport Officer.
Guards Division, "G".   Town Major, MAUREPAS.
Guards Division, "Q".   Town Major, COMBLES.

INSTRUCTIONS NO. 1 FOR SAILLISEL SECTOR.

Date.	Left Front.	Right Front.	Support.	Reserve.
March 12th.	2/C.G. in.	—	1/I.G. in.	—
13th.	2/C.G.	1/I.G. in.	3/C.G. in.	—
14th.	2/C.G.	1/I.G.	3/C.G.	2/G.G. in.
15th.	2/C.G.	1/I.G.	3/C.G.	2/G.G.
16th.	2/C.G. out. 3/C.G. in.	1/I.G.	3/C.G. out. 2/C.G. in.	2/G.G.
17th.	3/C.G.	1/I.G. out. 2/G.G. in.	2/C.G.	2/G.G. out. 1/I.G. in.
18th.	3/C.G.	2/G.G.	2/C.G.	1/I.G.
19th.	3/C.G.	2/G.G.	2/C.G.	1/I.G.
20th.	3/C.G. out. 2/C.G. in.	2/G.G.	2/C.G. out. 1/I.G. in.	1/I.G. out. 3/C.G. in.
21st.	2/C.G.	2/G.G. out. 1/I.G. in.	1/I.G. out. 2/G.G. in.	3/C.G.

2.   All details of relief will be arranged direct between
        O. C's. concerned.

3.   All movement must be by Platoons at 200 yards
        interval.

(2)

4. Completion of reliefs must be reported in Code to this Office.

5. Units moving into the Line will send on an advanced party of 1 N.C.O. per Company and per Battalion H.d., to take over Stores, etc.,

Units moving into Support or Reserve will send on a party to take over.

6. Final arrangements made for drawing and returning Gum Boots, Water Tins, etc., will be notified later.

7. There is a Foot-bath at COMBLES near the old Gum Boot Store for the Support Battalion and at MAUREPAS for the Reserve Battalion. Units must arrange direct with the N.C.O. in charge for the use of these Baths.

ACKNOWLEDGE.

Captain,

11th March 1917.

Brigade Major, 1st Guards Bde.,

SECRET.   1st G.B. No.1940/1.

2nd Bn. Grenadier Guards.   1st Bn. Irish Guards.
2nd Bn. Coldstream Guards.   Bde., Machine Gun Company.
3rd Bn. Coldstream Guards.   1st Guards T. M. Battery.

INSTRUCTIONS NO. 2 FOR SAILLISEL SECTOR.

Subject :- RETURNS.

1.   The following Returns will be rendered daily by the two Battalions in the Front Line :-

	Due Brigade H.Q.,
Morning Report (by wire)	8-30 A.M.
Intelligence Report by Orderly	10.0 A.M.
Evening Report (by wire)	3-30 P.M.
Casualty Report (by wire, in code, covering period 12 noon to 12 noon).	3.30 P.M.
Demand for R.E. Stores, etc. direct to 75th Field Coy., R.E.	8.0 P.M.

2.   The Machine Gun Company in the line will render an Intelligence Report to reach these H.Q., at 10 A.M. daily, also a Casualty Report - Nil Returns to be rendered.

3.   Battalions in the Camps and the Trench Mortar Battery will only render Casualty Returns if they have casualties to report.

4.   The Intelligence Report should be rendered under the following headings :-

   1. Operations - (Patrols and Sniping).
   2. Intelligence.
   3. Aircraft.
   4. Artillery.
   5. Work - Number of coils of wire put out to be stated.

   Map references should be given if possible. Approximate Map references are of great assistance but if they are only approximate, this fact should be stated.
   This report will cover the period from 8-30 A.M. to 8-30 AM.

5.   An outgoing Battalion must be careful to hand over the days Intelligence to the incoming Battalion.

6.   Situation Reports do not always show the true situation on the Battalion Front and an effort should be made to make them of some real value as a Situation Report.

7.   The capture of a prisoner must be wired at once to Brigade H.Q., the Regiment to which the prisoner belongs being stated.
   Prisoners will be sent direct to Divnl. H.Q.,
   Units are reminded that documents are only to be taken off Officers when captured.
   Implements such as knives should be taken away put prisoners medals, valuables, pay-books, are not to be taken from them.

11th March 1917.   Captain,
                                          Brigade Major, 1st Guards Brigade.

SECRET.   1st G.B. No.1940/1.

2nd Bn. Grenadier Guards.   1st Bn. Irish Guards,
2nd Bn. Coldstream Guards.   Bde., Machine Gun Company,
3rd Bn. Coldstream Guards.   1st Guards T. M. Battery.

INSTRUCTIONS NO. 2 FOR BAILLEUL SECTOR.

Subject :- RETURNS.

1. The following Returns will be rendered daily by the two Battalions in the Front Line :-

	Due Brigade H.Q.
Morning Report (by wire)	8-30 A.M.
Intelligence Report by Orderly	10.0 A.M.
Evening Report (by wire)	5-30 P.M.
Casualty Report (by wire, in code, covering period 12 noon to 12 noon).	6.30 P.M.
Demand for R.E. Stores, etc. direct to 75th Field Coy., R.E.	6.0 P.M.

2. The Machine Gun Company in the line will render an Intelligence Report to reach these H.Q., at 10 A.M. daily, also a Casualty Report - Nil Returns to be rendered.

3. Battalions in the Camps and the Trench Mortar Battery will only render Casualty Returns if they have casualties to report.

4. The Intelligence Report should be rendered under the following headings :-

   1. Operations - (Patrols and Sniping).
   2. Intelligence.
   3. Aircraft.
   4. Artillery.
   5. Work - Number of coils of wire put out to be stated.

   Map references should be given if possible. Approximate Map references are of great assistance but if they are only approximate, this fact should be stated.
   This report will cover the period from 8-30 A.M. to 8-30 AM.

5. An outgoing Battalion must be careful to hand over the days Intelligence to the incoming Battalion.

6. Situation Reports do not always show the true situation on the Battalion Front and an effort should be made to make them of some real value as a Situation Report.

7. The capture of a prisoner must be wired at once to Brigade H.Q., the regiment to which the prisoner belongs being stated.
   Prisoners will be sent direct to Divnl. H.Q.,
   Units are reminded that documents are only to be taken off Officers when captured.
   Implements such as knives should be taken away but prisoners medals, valuables, pay-books, are not to be taken from them.

11th March 1917.   Captain,
                                 Brigade Major, 1st Guards Brigade.

S E C R E T.   1st G.B. No.1040/1.

2nd Bn. Grenadier Guards.   1st Bn. Irish Guards.
2nd Bn. Coldstream Guards.   Bde., Machine Gun Company.
3rd Bn. Coldstream Guards.   1st Guards T. M. Battery.

INSTRUCTIONS No. 2 FOR BATTALIONS IN LINE.

Subject :- RETURNS.

1. The following Returns will be rendered daily by the two Battalions in the Front Line :-

                                                   To Brigade H.Q.
   Morning Report (by wire)   7-30 A.M.
   Intelligence Report by Orderly   10.0 A.M.
   Evening Report (by wire)   2-30 P.M.
   Casualty Report (by wire, in code, covering
       period 12 noon to 12 noon).   3.30 P.M.
   Demand for R.E. Stores, etc. direct to
       76th Field Coy., R.E.   5.0 P.M.

2. The Machine Gun Company in the line will render an Intelligence Report to reach these H.Q., at 10 A.M. daily, also a Casualty Report - Nil Returns to be rendered.

3. Battalions in the Camps and the Trench Mortar Battery will only render Casualty Returns if they have casualties to report.

4. The Intelligence Report should be rendered under the following headings :-

   1. Operations - (Patrols and Sniping).
   2. Intelligence.
   3. Aircraft.
   4. Artillery.
   5. Work - Number of coils of wire put out to be stated.

   Map references should be given if possible. Approximate Map references are of great assistance but if they are only approximate, this fact should be stated.
   This report will cover the period from 8-30 A.M. to 8-30 A.M.

5. An outgoing Battalion must be careful to hand over the days Intelligence to the incoming Battalion.

6. Situation Reports do not always show the true situation on the Battalion Front and an effort should be made to make them of some real value as a Situation Report.

7. The capture of a prisoner must be wired at once to Brigade H.Q., the Regiment to which the prisoner belongs being stated.
   Prisoners will be sent direct to Divnl. H.Q.,
   Units are reminded that documents are only to be taken off officers when captured.
   Implements such as knives should be taken away but prisoners medals, valuables, pay-books, are not to be taken from them.

11th March 1917.   Brigade Major, 1st Guards Brigade.
                                                        Captain,

1st Guards Brigade Intelligence Report.

8 a.m. Mch. 13th to 8 a.m. Mch. 14th.

OPERATIONS.

Very little rifle or Machine Gun fire. We fired a few Rifle Grenades in retaliation for German Rifle Grenades.

INTELLIGENCE.

Work in progress was noticed at U 3 c 4.5. A dugout and an O.P. are suspected here.

Various other small parties of Germans were seen at different times at U 8 d 7.2. and in the vicinity of ROCQUIGNY.

A very large number of Very Lights were put up from the German Front and Support Lines. Green lights were apparently sent up as a Signal for the Artillery to lengthen range and Green and Red for the Artillery to cease fire.

Our wire in front of No.1, 2, 3, 4 & 5 Posts was observed to be very weak. It consists of a continuous row of French wire without any barbed wire.

AIRCRAFT.

At about 6 p.m. 5 small German Tractor Biplanes were flying at an altitude of from 2000 to 3000 ft. over SAILLY SAILLISEL. They remained in the vicinity for half-an-hour and were fired upon by Machine Guns from the ground without effect.

ARTILLERY.

The area chiefly shelled was SAILLY WOOD. There was a good deal of indiscriminate shelling over the remainder of the Brigade Sector.

MACHINE GUNS.

Hostile Machine Guns fired short bursts with intervals of about an hour throughout the night down the main SAILLY - BAPAUME Road.

Captain,
for Brigade Major, 1st Guards Brigade.

S E C R E T.

1st Guards Brigade Order No.106.

Ref. Map - COMBLES 1/10,000.   March 14th, 1917.

1.   All indications show that an enemy withdrawal on our front will start in the next few days.

2.   Active patrolling will be maintained by Battn's., in the line.

3.   If patrols report that part or all of the enemy front line has been vacated, this line will be occupied by Posts, but no further advance will be made without reference to Brigade H.Q.,

4.   On receipt of Orders the following procedure will be adopted :-

A. (i)   The two Battn's. in the line will each detail two Coy's. to act as Advanced Guards and make good the line - Level crossing U.16.a.5.2. along Road to U.10.c.8.1. thence along line FERDINAND - BULGAR Trench to U.3.d.8.5. thence to N.E. corner of LOON Copse.

   (ii) Southern Boundary of Brigade Area is the line of the Railway in U.15.d. and b. and U.16.a.

         Northern Boundary of Brigade Area is a line drawn from U.8.a.8.2. 100 yards N. of HAMMER Copse to N.E. corner of LOON Copse.

   (iii) The 2nd Guards Brigade and 60th Infantry Brigade on our right and left respectively will be sending out similar and simultaneous Advanced Guards directed on the general line GOVERNMENT Farm LOON Copse and the COPSE in O.34.c.

B.   The advance will be carried out as follows :-

   (i)   One Advanced Guard Coy. from each Battn., will push forward preceded by patrols and supported by the other Coy. of it's Battn.,

   (ii) Two spurs run Eastwards from our line and Advanced Guard Coy's. will work forward along those spurs.

   (iii) The advance will be carried out in two bounds -

         (a) From enemy's and our present Front line to the line COBURG - GOTHA Trench.

         (b) From the COBURG - GOTHA Trench line to the final objective mentioned in para A. (i).

   (iv) On reaching objectives Advanced Guard Coy's. will gain touch with the Coy's. on their flanks. No advance from the first to the final objective will be made until this touch has first been gained   every effort will be made by leading Coy's. and Patrols to advance from the first towards the final objective at the same time as Coy's. on the flanks.

(v) The portions of the final objective which must first be made good are -

U.10.c.8.0. - U.10.c 3.6 for Right Battn., leading Coy.,
U.4.c.0.0. - U 3 d 8.9 with a Post pushed forward to the N E. corner of LOON COPSE ─ ─ ─ ─ ─ , for Left Battn., leading Coy.,

(vi) Companies must be distributed in depth throughout. No attack on a large scale will be attempted but minor opposition must be dealt with by strong Patrols or by Supporting Coy's. of Advanced Guard.

(vii) Objectives when gained will be consolidated. The object to be aimed at is the establishing of a line of outposts by leading Advanced Guard Coy's. on the two spurs at the points mentioned in B. (v).

(viii) As soon as leading Advanced Guard Coy's. are clear of enemy front line, this line will be occupied by Support Coy's. of Advanced Guard. Similarly the COBURG - GOTHA Trench Line will be occupied by Support Coy's. as soon as clear of leading Coy's. of Advanced Guard. Support Coy's. will not advance beyond the COBURG - GOTHA Line unless required to Support leading Coy's. in dealing with minor opposition or to protect their flanks. COBURG - GOTHA Trench must be consolidated as soon as occupied by Support Coy's. of Advanced Guard.

(ix) Coy's. detailed to go forward will carry -

2 bombs per man.
4 sandbags "
80% of men will carry shovels.
25 flares per Company.

C. (i) From Zero (i.e. the hour at which Advanced Guards will be ordered to push forward) the two Coy's. of each Battn., detailed to act as Advanced Guard will come under the Orders of the Senior Commdg., Officer in the line.

(ii) His H.Q., will be established at SAILLY Church as soon as possible after the order to advance is received.

(iii) (a) Coy's. detailed as Advanced Guard will each send two Runners to report at the CHURCH.

(b) Battn's. in the line will each detail 2 Signallers with flags and discs and 1 telephone to report at the CHURCH.
(c) The Bde., Signalling Officer will detail 1 Sgt. and 4 Signallers to report at the CHURCH.
(d) O.C., Left Group will detail 1 Officer and Signallers to report at the CHURCH.
(e) The Coy. H.Q., in CANE Alley must be cleared so as to accommodate Orderlies, etc., of those H.Q.,

(iv) From Zero all messages and reports will be sent by all Advanced Guard Coy's. direct to this Officer.

(v) As soon as leading troops report COBURG – GOTHA Trench clear or as soon as this is soon to be occupied by our troops, this Officer will move his H.Q., forward to about U.15.a.4,7., whence it is hoped that Visual will be maintained with leading Coy's.

(vi) The Report Centre at SAILLY Church will be taken over by 1 Sgt. and 4 Signallers from Brigade H.Q., as soon as the Advanced Guard Commander moves forward, and a line will be maintained by Bde., Signalling Officer forward to U.15.a.4.7.

(vii) Care will be taken not to establish a Visual Signalling Station too near any point selected by the Artillery Officer for an O.P.

D. **ARTILLERY.**

(i) Batteries are being pushed up to the vicinity of SAILLISEL so as to cover the final objective.

(ii) The Artillery Officer with Advanced Guard Commander will deal with all Artillery requirement.

(iii) A F.O.O. will be detailed by O.C., Left Group to advance along the spur allotted to Left Battn., Advanced Guard, and this Officer will help to deal with any Artillery requirements on that flank.

E. **MACHINE GUNS & TRENCH MORTAR BTY.** will be prepared to push forward guns as ordered after objectives have been gained.

F. **75TH COY., R.E.** with the exception of 16 men will be employed on pushing one main track Eastwards from BULLET Cross Roads. As soon as situation permits 4 men will be sent up to each Advanced Guard Coy. to search dug-outs etc., for mines.

G. **Sapping Platoons** at MOUCHOIR COPSE will remain in their present positions. They may be required for carrying or consolidation.

H. **Reserve Coy's. of Battn's. in the line –**

(i) The two Coy's. of Battn's. in the line will occupy our present Front and Support lines as soon as these are clear of Advanced Guard Troops. The improvement of these lines must be pushed on with.

(ii) These Reserve Coy's. may under cover of darkness be pushed forward to consolidate objectives gained.

I. **Support and Reserve Battn's.** will be prepared to move at short notice. Support Battn., will probably be required to find a Company to assist in Road making.

(4)

J. **Brigade & Battn., H.Q.,**

    (i) Brigade H.Q., will move as soon as final objectives have been reported occupied to the present Right Battn.,H.Q., at U.19.a.8.8. Left Group Artillery H.Q., will also move to this point at the same time.

    (ii) Left Battn., H.Q., will not move forward.

    (iii) Right Battn., H.Q., will move to their Coy. H.Q., just S.W. of BULLET Cross Roads.

    (iv) All H.Q., must be in possession of their ground sheets for communication with Aeroplane.

K. **MEDICAL Arrangements.**

    Stretcher cases will be evacuated from the Right Battn., Aid Post at U.19.a.8.6.

L. **MISCELLANEOUS.**

    (i) All ranks will be forbidden to enter any enemy dug-out until it has been pronounced safe by R.E.

    (ii) In all Reports the Map referred to should be stated.

    (iii) Prisoners will be sent direct to Divnl. H.Q.,

    (iv) Gum-boots, packs, great-coats and other kit not required by advancing troops will be stored under Platoon arrangements and one man left in charge.

    (v) Supplies for Advanced Guard Troops will be sent up after objectives have been reached, under Bde., arrangements.

    (vi) Wire cutters must be carried by proportion of Advanced Troops.

    (vii) Flares will be lit when asked for by Aeroplane.

The Orders laid down in para's A to L above will be carried out on receipt of message "Advanced Guard Forward" followed by Zero hour in Code.

    ACKNOWLEDGE.

    ****

                                                  Captain,
                      Brigade Major, 1st Guards Brigade.

Issued to Signals at 9 p.m.

Copies to :-

2nd Bn. Grenadier Guards.	2nd Guards Brigade.
2nd Bn. Coldstream Guards.	60th Infantry Brigade.
3rd Bn. Coldstream Guards.	Left Group, G.D.A.,
1st Bn. Irish Guards.	75th Field Coy., R.E.
Bde., Machine Gun Company.	O.C., 2/Cold.Gds. Sapping Platoon.
1st Guards T. M. Battery.	O.C., 1/Irish Gds.
Guards Division.	Staff Captain.
	O.C., Signals.

SECRET.

        1st Guards Brigade   Order No.106.

Ref. Map - COMBLES 1/10,000.   March 14th, 1917.

1. All indications show that an enemy withdrawal on our front will start in the next few days.

2. Active patrolling will be maintained by Battn's., in the line.

3. If patrols report that part or all of the enemy front line has been vacated, this line will be occupied by Posts, but no further advance will be made without reference to Brigade H.Q.,

4. On receipt of Orders the following procedure will be adopted :-

   A. (i) The two Battn's. in the line will each detail two Coy's. to act as Advanced Guards and make good the line - Level crossing U.16.a.5.2. along Road to U.10.c.8.1. thence along line FERDINAND - BULGAR Trench to U.3.d.5.5. thence to N.E. corner of LOON Copse.

     (ii) Southern Boundary of Brigade Area is the line of the Railway in U.15.d. and b. and U.16.a.

     Northern Boundary of Brigade Area is a line drawn from U.8.a.8.2. 100 yards N. of HAMMER Copse to N.E. corner of LOON Copse.

    (iii) The 2nd Guards Brigade and 60th Infantry Brigade on our right and left respectively will be sending out similar and simultaneous Advanced Guards directed on the general line GOVERNMENT Farm LOON Copse and the COPSE in O.34.c.

   B. The advance will be carried out as follows :-

     (i) One Advanced Guard Coy. from each Battn., will push forward preceded by patrols and supported by the other Coy. of it's Battn.,

    (ii) Two spurs run Eastwards from our line and Advanced Guard Coy's. will work forward along those spurs.

   (iii) The advance will be carried out in two bounds -

       (a) From enemy's and our present Front line to the line COBURG - GOTHA Trench.

       (b) From the COBURG - GOTHA Trench line to the final objective mentioned in para A. (i).

    (iv) On reaching objectives Advanced Guard Coy's. will gain touch with the Coy's. on their flanks. No advance from the first to the final objective will be made until this touch has first been gained   every effort will be made by leading Coy's. and Patrols to advance from the first towards the final objective at the same time as Coy's. on the flanks.

(2)

(v) The portions of the final objective which must first be made good are -

U.10.c.8.0. - U.10.c.3.6 for Right Battn., leading Coy.
U.4.c.0.0. - U.3.d.8.9 with a Post pushed forward to the N E corner of LOON COPSE, for Left Battn., leading Coy.

(vi) Companies must be distributed in depth throughout. No attack on a large scale will be attempted but minor opposition must be dealt with by strong Patrols or by Supporting Coy's. of Advanced Guard.

(vii) Objectives when gained will be consolidated. The object to be aimed at is the establishing of a line of outposts by leading Advanced Guard Coy's. on the two spurs at the points mentioned in B (v).

(viii) As soon as leading Advanced Guard Coy's. are clear of enemy front line, this line will be occupied by Support Coy's. of Advanced Guard. Similarly the COBURG - GOTHA Trench Line will be occupied by Support Coy's. as soon as clear of leading Coy's. of Advanced Guard. Support Coy's. will not advance beyond the COBURG - GOTHA Line unless required to Support leading Coy's. in dealing with minor opposition or to protect their flanks. COBURG - GOTHA Trench must be consolidated as soon as occupied by Support Coy's. of Advanced Guard.

(ix) Coy's. detailed to go forward will carry -

2 bombs per man.
4 sandbags "
80% of men will carry shovels.
25 flares per Company.

C. (i) From Zero (i.e. the hour at which Advanced Guards will be ordered to push forward) the two Coy's. of each Battn. detailed to act as Advanced Guard will come under the Orders of the Senior Commdg., Officer in the line.

(ii) His H.Q., will be established at SAILLY Church as soon as possible after the order to advance is received.

(iii) (a) Coy's. detailed as Advanced Guard will each send two Runners to report at the CHURCH.

(b) Battn's. in the line will each detail 2 Signallers with flags and discs and 1 telephone to report at the CHURCH.
(c) The Bde., Signalling Officer will detail 1 Sgt. and 4 Signallers to report at the CHURCH.
(d) O.C., Left Group will detail 1 Officer and Signallers to report at the CHURCH
(e) The Coy. H.Q., in CANE Alley must be cleared so as to accommodate Orderlies, etc., of these H.Q.,

(iv) From Zero all messages and reports will be sent by all Advanced Guard Coy's. direct to this Officer.

(v) As soon as leading troops report COBURG – GOTHA Trench clear or as soon as this is soon to be occupied by our troops, this Officer will move his H.Q., forward to about U.15.a.4.7., whence it is hoped that Visual will be maintained with leading Coy's.

(vi) The Report Centre at SAILLY Church will be taken over by 1 Sgt. and 4 Signallers from Brigade H.Q., as soon as the Advanced Guard Commander moves forward, and a line will be maintained by Bde., Signalling Officer forward to U.15.a.4.7.

(vii) Care will be taken not to establish a Visual Signalling Station too near any point selected by the Artillery Officer for an O.P.

D. **ARTILLERY.**

(i) Batteries are being pushed up to the vicinity of SAILLISEL so as to cover the final objective.

(ii) The Artillery Officer with Advanced Guard Commander will deal with all Artillery requirement.

(iii) A F.O.O. will be detailed by O.C., Left Group to advance along the spur allotted to Left Battn., Advanced Guard, and this Officer will help to deal with any Artillery requirements on that flank.

E. **MACHINE GUNS & TRENCH MORTAR BTY.** will be prepared to push forward guns as ordered after objectives have been gained.

F. **75TH COY., R.E.** with the exception of 16 men will be employed on pushing one main track Eastwards from BULLET Cross Roads. As soon as situation permits 4 men will be sent up to each Advanced Guard Coy. to search dug-outs etc., for mines.

G. **Sapping Platoons** at MOUCHOIR COPSE will remain in their present positions. They may be required for carrying or consolidation.

H. **Reserve Coy's, of Battn's. in the line –**

(i) The two Coy's. of Battn's. in the line will occupy our present Front and Support lines as soon as these are clear of Advanced Guard Troops. The improvement of these lines must be pushed on with.

(ii) These Reserve Coy's. may under cover of darkness be pushed forward to consolidate objectives gained.

I. **Support and Reserve Battn's.** will be prepared to move at short notice. Support Battn., will probably be required to find a Company to assist in Road making.

(4)

J. **Brigade & Battn., H.Q.,**

   (i) Brigade H.Q., will move as soon as final objectives have been reported occupied to the present Right Battn., H.Q., at U.19.a.8.8. Left Group Artillery H.Q., will also move to this point at the same time.

   (ii) Left Battn., H.Q., will not move forward.

   (iii) Right Battn., H.Q., will move to their Coy. H.Q., just S.W. of BULLET Cross Roads.

   (iv) All H.Q., must be in possession of their ground sheets for communication with Aeroplane.

K. **MEDICAL Arrangements.**

   Stretcher cases will be evacuated from the Right Battn., Aid Post at U.19.a.8.6.

L. **MISCELLANEOUS.**

   (i) All ranks will be forbidden to enter any enemy dug-out until it has been pronounced safe by R.E.

   (ii) In all Reports the Map referred to should be stated.

   (iii) Prisoners will be sent direct to Divnl. H.Q.,

   (iv) Gum-boots, packs, great-coats and other kit not required by advancing troops will be stored under Platoon arrangements and one man left in charge.

   (v) Supplies for Advanced Guard Troops will be sent up after objectives have been reached, under Bde., arrangements.

   (vi) Wire cutters must be carried by proportion of Advanced Troops.

   (vii) Flares will be lit when asked for by Aeroplane.

   The Orders laid down in para's A to L above will be carried out on receipt of message "Advanced Guard Forward" followed by Zero hour in Code.

   ACKNOWLEDGE.
   ****

                                                        Captain,
                                       Brigade Major, 1st Guards Brigade.

Issued to Signals at 9 p.m.

Copies to :-
   2nd Bn. Grenadier Guards.   2nd Guards Brigade.
   2nd Bn. Coldstream Guards.   60th Infantry Brigade.
   3rd Bn. Coldstream Guards.   Left Group, G.D.A.,
   1st Bn. Irish Guards.   75th Field Coy., R.E.
   Bde., Machine Gun Company.   O.C., 2/Cold.Gds. Sapping Platoon.
   1st Guards T. M. Battery.   O.C., 1/Irish Gds.
   Guards Division.   Staff Captain.
                                      O.C., Signals.

SECRET.

1st Guards Brigade Order No. 107.

17th March 1917.

1. From the night of 17th inst., inclusive the Brigade will be distributed as follows :-

   (a) The out-posts covering the Brigade front will be found by one Battalion.

   (b) 1 Battalion will be in Support.

   (c) 2 Battalions will be in Reserve (1 in COMBLES Area and 1 at MAUREPAS).

   (d) 3 Guns of Machine Gun Company will be in the out-post line.
   4 Guns of Machine Gun Company in Reserve at HAIE WOOD.
   Remainder of Guns of Machine Gun Company will be in Support.

2. On the night of 17th, the 3rd Bn. Coldstream Guards will take over the whole of the out-post line COBURG - GOTHA - BRUNSWICK Trench from U 15 b 6.1. including BEYREUTH Trench, to U 8 b 3.4.

3. The 2nd Bn. Grenadier Guards will be in Support and will take over the positions of the present Reserve Coy's. of the 3rd Bn. Coldstream Guards and the Support and Reserve Coy. of the 1st Bn. Irish Guards.
   Battalion H.Q., will be at the HEBULE.

4. Details and times of relief will be issued later.

   ACKNOWLEDGE.

Captain,

Brigade Major, 1st Guards Brigade.

Issued to Signals at 4-30 a.m.

Copies to :-

   2nd Bn. Grenadier Guards.
   2nd Bn. Coldstream Guards.
   3rd Bn. Coldstream Guards.
   1st Bn. Irish Guards.
   Bde., Machine Gun Company.
   Bde., Trench Mortar Battery.
   Left Group, G.D.A.
   Guards Division.
   2nd Guards Brigade.
   3rd Guards Brigade.
   75th Field Coy., R.E.

SECRET.   Copy No. 12

In continuation
of
1st Guards Brigade Order No. 107.

17th March 1917.

Instructions as to details and times of relief as follows :-

1.   On completion of relief Battalions will be disposed as follows :-

<u>2nd Bn. Grenadier Guards</u> (Support Battn.,)
    Battn., H.Q., and 6 Platoons at the HEBULE.
                    2 Platoons at SOUTH Copse.) Known as Left
    1 Company in old German Front Line from) Support Company.
    U 15 c 1.7. to U 14 b 9.4.   )
    1 Company (1 platoon U 15 c 1.2½.   ) Known as
              (1 platoon U 14 d 9.5.   ) Right
              (1 platoon BETTYE RESERVE.   ) Support
              (1 platoon about U 19 b 6.8.) Company.

<u>3rd Bn. Coldstream Guards.</u>
    The line COBURG - GOTHA - BRUNSWICK Trench from U 15 b 6.2. -
U 8 b 3.4. including BAYREUTH Trench and Advanced Posts in POLE
Avenue and FERDINAND Trench.

<u>2nd Bn. Coldstream Guards.</u> (Reserve in COMBLES Area).
    Battn., H.Q., and 1 Company in FREGICOURT.
                    1 Company in COMBLES.
                    1 Company in HAIE WOOD.
                    1 Company HAIE WOOD - COMBLES Road about
                      T 23 c 1.0.

<u>1st Bn. Irish Guards.</u> (Reserve MAUREPAS).

2.   The 2nd Bn. Grenadier Guards will relieve [2 Coys of] 3rd Bn. Coldstream
Guards as follows :-

        2 Coy's. and Battn.,H.Q., at HEBULE. Relief to be complete
by 7 p.m.
        Leading Company of 2nd Bn. Grenadier Guards not to pass HAIE
WOOD before 5-45 p.m.

        The 2nd Bn. Grenadier Guards will relieve [2 Coys of] 1st Bn. Irish
Guards as follows :-

        1 Company to relieve Left Support Company of 1st Bn. Irish
Guards and to be clear of 1st Bn. Irish Guards Battn., H.Q., by
5-30 p.m.
        1 Company to relieve Right Support Company of 1st Bn. Irish
Guards. Head of Company not to pass 1st Bn. Irish Guards H.Q.,
before 6-15 p.m.

        Details of relief of 1st Bn. Irish Guards Outpost Coy's.
by 3rd Bn. Coldstream Guards to be arranged direct

3.   The 2nd Bn. Grenadier Guards will send on an advanced party
of not less than 1 N.C.O. per Company and 1 Officer and 1 N.C.O.
for Battn., H.Q., to take over Stores, etc.,

        Reference this Office No.1933/3 of the 15th inst.,
INSTRUCTIONS for SAILLISEL Sector.

        The supply of water and rations will be as follows :-

    For Outpost Battalion (3/Cold.Gds.) the same as for Right Battn.,
(1/Irish Gds).

1.

For Support Battn., (2/Gren.Gds.).
    Battn., H.Q., and 2 Coy's. at HEBULE by Train to HEBULE.
    (Due to leave COMBLES at 4-30 p.m.)
    2 Coy's. in the line.
    Rations by limbers from COMBLES to 3rd Bn. Coldstream Guards H.Q.,

    Water.   50 full water tins will be available at 3rd Bn. Coldstream Guards H.Q., (U 19 a 8.6.).
    (Two limbers have been allotted under Bde. arrangement to be at Railhead at COMBLES at 2-30 p.m. for these rations).

5.   3rd Bn. Coldstream Guards will arrange to hand over all full water tins to 2nd Bn. Grenadier Guards on relief at the HEBULE and SOUTH Copse.
    100 full water tins will be available for these 3rd Bn. Coldstream Guards Coy's. at H.Q., 1st Bn. Irish Guards and a further supply will be issued if necessary on application to this Office.

6.   Reference INSTRUCTIONS on SAILLISEL Sector issued under this Office No.1933/3 of 15th inst.,
    The following alterations are made :-

    For Right Battn., read Outpost Battn.,
    For Left Battn., read Support Battn.,
    For Support Battn., read Reserve Battn.,

7.   Details of Guides will be arranged by Battalions direct.

ACKNOWLEDGE.

                                          Captain,
                Brigade Major, 1st Guards Brigade.

Issued to Signals at 1-15 p.m.

    Copies to :-

        2nd Bn. Grenadier Guards.
        2nd Bn. Coldstream Guards.
        3rd Bn. Coldstream Guards.
        1st Bn. Irish Guards.
        Bde., Machine Gun Company.
        Bde., Trench Mortar Battery.
        Left Group, G.D.A.
        Guards Division.
        2nd Guards Brigade.
        3rd Guards Brigade.
        75th Field Coy., R.E.

SECRET.   Copy No. 13

In continuation
of
1st Guards Brigade Order No. 107.

                                                                17th March 1917.

Instructions as to details and times of relief as follows :-

1.   On completion of relief Battalions will be disposed as follows :-

2nd Bn. Grenadier Guards (Support Battn.,)
    Battn., H.Q., and 6 Platoons at the HEBULE.
                    2 Platoons at SOUTH Copse.) Known as Left
    1 Company in old German Front Line from) Support Company.
    U 15 c 1.7. to U 14 b 9.4.   )
    1 Company (1 platoon U 15 c 1.2½.   ) Known as
              (1 platoon U 14 d 9.5.   ) Right
              (1 platoon BETTYE RESERVE.   ) Support
              (1 platoon about U 19 b 6.8.   ) Company.

3rd Bn. Coldstream Guards.
    The line COBURG - GOTHA - BRUNSWICK Trench from U 15 b 6.2. -
    U 8 b 3.4. including BAYREUTH Trench and Advanced posts in POLE
    Avenue and FERDINAND Trench.

2nd Bn. Coldstream Guards. (Reserve in COMBLES Area).
    Battn., H.Q., and 1 Company in FREGICOURT.
                    1 Company in COMBLES.
                    1 Company in HAIE WOOD.
                    1 Company HAIE WOOD - COMBLES Road about
                    T 23 c 1.0.

1st Bn. Irish Guards. (Reserve MAUREPAS).

2.   The 2nd Bn. Grenadier Guards will relieve 2 Coys of 3rd Bn. Coldstream Guards as follows :-

        2 Coy's. and Battn.,H.Q., at HEBULE.   Relief to be complete by 7 p.m.
        Leading Company of 2nd Bn. Grenadier Guards not to pass HAIE WOOD before 5-45 p.m.

        The 2nd Bn. Grenadier Guards will relieve 2 Coys of 1st Bn. Irish Guards as follows :-

        1 Company to relieve Left Support Company of 1st Bn. Irish Guards and to be clear of 1st Bn. Irish Guards H.Q., by 5-30 p.m.
        1 Company to relieve Right Support Company of 1st Bn. Irish Guards. Head of Company not to pass 1st Bn. Irish Guards H.Q., before 6-15 p.m.

        Details of relief of 1st Bn. Irish Guards Outpost Coy's. by 3rd Bn. Coldstream Guards to be arranged direct

3.   The 2nd Bn. Grenadier Guards will send on an advanced party of not less than 1 N.C.O. per Company and 1 Officer and 1 N.C.O. for Battn., H.Q., to take over Stores, etc.,

        Reference this Office No.1933/3 of the 15th inst., INSTRUCTIONS for SAILLISEL Sector.

        The supply of water and rations will be as follows :-

        For Outpost Battalion (3/Cold.Gds.) the same as for Right Battn., (1/Irish Gds).

1.

For Support Battn., (2/Gren.Gds.).
   Battn., H.Q., and 2 Coy's. at HEBULE by Train to HEBULE.
   (Due to leave COMBLES at 4-30 p.m.)
   2 Coy's. in the line.
   Rations by limbers from COMBLES to 3rd Bn. Coldstream Guards H.Q.,

   Water.   50 full water tins will be available at 3rd Bn. Coldstream Guards H.Q., (U 19 a 8.6.).
   (Two limbers have been allotted under Bde. arrangement to be at Railhead at COMBLES at 2-30 p.m. for these rations).

5.   3rd Bn. Coldstream Guards will arrange to hand over all full water tins to 2nd Bn. Grenadier Guards on relief at the HEBULE and SOUTH Copse.
   100 full water tins will be available for these 3rd Bn. Coldstream Guards Coy's. at H.Q., 1st Bn. Irish Guards and a further supply will be issued if necessary on application to this Office.

6.   Reference INSTRUCTIONS on SAILLISEL Sector issued under this Office No.1933/3 of 15th inst.,
   The following alterations are made :-

   For Right Battn., read Outpost Battn.,
   For Left Battn., read Support Battn.,
   For Support Battn., read Reserve Battn.,

7.   Details of Guides will be arranged by Battalions direct.

ACKNOWLEDGE.

                                                Captain,
                        Brigade Major, 1st Guards Brigade.

Issued to Signals at 1-15 p.m.

   Copies to :-

      2nd Bn. Grenadier Guards.
      2nd Bn. Coldstream Guards.
      3rd Bn. Coldstream Guards.
      1st Bn. Irish Guards.
      Bde., Machine Gun Company.
      Bde., Trench Mortar Battery.
      Left Group, G.D.A.
      Guards Division.
      2nd Guards Brigade.
      3rd Guards Brigade.
      75th Field Coy., R.E.

SECRET.

1st Guards Brigade Order No. 107.

17th March 1917.

1. From the night of 17th inst., inclusive the Brigade will be distributed as follows :-

   (a) The out-posts covering the Brigade front will be found by one Battalion.

   (b) 1 Battalion will be in Support.

   (c) 2 Battalions will be in Reserve (1 in COMBLES Area and 1 at MAUREPAS).

   (d) 3 Guns of Machine Gun Company will be in the out-post line. 4 Guns of Machine Gun Company in Reserve at HAIE WOOD. Remainder of Guns of Machine Gun Company will be in Support.

2. On the night of 17th, the 3rd Bn. Coldstream Guards will take over the whole of the out-post line COBURG - GOTHA - BRUNSWICK Trench from U 15 b 6.1. including BEYREUTH Trench, to U 8 b 3.4.

3. The 2nd Bn. Grenadier Guards will be in Support and will take over the positions of the present Reserve Coy's. of the 3rd Bn. Coldstream Guards and the Support and Reserve Coy. of the 1st Bn. Irish Guards.
Battalion H.Q., will be at the HEBULE.

4. Details and times of relief will be issued later.

ACKNOWLEDGE.

Captain,

Brigade Major, 1st Guards Brigade.

Issued to Signals at 4-30 a.m.

Copies to :-

2nd Bn. Grenadier Guards.
2nd Bn. Coldstream Guards.
3rd Bn. Coldstream Guards.
1st Bn. Irish Guards.
Bde., Machine Gun Company.
Bde., Trench Mortar Battery.
Left Group, G.D.A.
Guards Division.
2nd Guards Brigade.
3rd Guards Brigade.
75th Field Coy., R.E.

SECRET.   Copy No. 17.

1st Guards Brigade Operation Order No.108.
****

                                                                    18th March 1917.

1. **SITUATION.**

   (a)   1st Guards Brigade is holding a line BRUNSWICK Trench - POLE Trench - FERDINAND Trench with standing patrols in HAMMER Copse - BULGAR Trench - Cross Roads U 10 c and d central.

   (b)   1st Guards Brigade is in touch with 2nd Guards Brigade on the Right in BATOCKI Trench and at Cross Roads U 10 c and d and with 60th Brigade on the Left at the N.W. end of HAMMER Copse.

   (c)   The enemy are retiring rapidly on a line BUS - LECHELLE - EQUANCOURT. At present the exact line that he is holding is not known.

2.   2nd Bn. Grenadier Guards will relieve 3rd Bn. Coldstream Guards in the outpost line to-night. O.C., 2nd Bn. Grenadier Guards will be O.C., Outposts.

3.   Details and hour of relief will be arranged between C. O's. concerned.

4.   O.C., Outposts will establish a line of picquets on an approximate line HAMMER Copse - POLE Trench U 9 b 3.4. - FERDINAND Trench between U 10 a 0.1. and U 10 c 2.3. - Quarry U 16 a 2.3.

       Groups will be established on an approximate line LOON Copse - BULGAR Trench to the junction of BULGAR Trench and FERDINAND Trench U 10 a 2.7½. - Cross Roads U 10 c and d thence Southwards along the Road through U 16 a and c to U 16 a 4½.2½. A standing patrol will be established at U 10 d 9.6. (Junction of Road running East from STAR Cross Roads with BATOCKI Trench).

       Support Line will be established on a line PLANET Trench - BRUNSWICK Trench - GOTHA Trench - COBURG Trench.

       The line of defence will be the Support Line.

5.   The Brigade Boundaries will remain as before on the right the line of the Railway running from U 15 d in an Easterly direction - on the left a line running from the junction of PLANET and BRUNSWICK Trenches, U 8 b 3.3. past the North Easterly edge of HAMMER Copse and LOON Copse.

       Communication will be maintained with 2nd Guards Brigade on the Right and 60th Brigade on the left.

6.   O.C., Outposts will arrange for active patrolling of LE MESNIL - OPAKA Trench - AHCHISE Trench, but patrols will not proceed further than 1,000 yards in an Easterly direction from the line of Groups.

7.   O.C., Outposts will arrange for systematic observation of the high ground East of LE MESNIL.

2.

8. O.C., Outposts will establish his H.Q., in the vicinity of Road junction U 14 b 9½.8½., and will report which point he selected as H.Q.,

9. On relief 3rd Bn. Coldstream Guards will become the Battalion in Support. Their dispositions will be similar to those at present occupied by 2nd Bn. Grenadier Guards with the exception of Battalion H.Q., which will remain at U 19 a 8.8.

10. The positions of Brigade H.Q., and Other Units of the 1st Guards Brigade will remain as at present.

11. Administrative details will be communicated by the Staff Captain.

ACKNOWLEDGE.

J S Dyer.
Captain,
Brigade Major, 1st Guards Brigade.

Issued through Signals at 3-15 p.m.

Copy No. 1 2nd Bn. Grenadier Guards.
2 2nd Bn. Coldstream Guards.
3 3rd Bn. Coldstream Guards.
4 1st Bn. Irish Guards.
5 Bde., Machine Gun Company.
6 Bde., Trench Mortar Battery.
7 Left Group, G.D.A.
8 Guards Division.
9 2nd Guards Brigade.
10 3rd Guards Brigade.
11 60th Infantry Brigade.
12 75th Field Coy., R.E.
13 9th Field Ambulance.
14 Staff Captain.
15 O.C., Signals.
16 - 20 Retained.

SECRET.   Copy No. 18

1st Guards Brigade Operation Order No. 109.

19th March 1917.

1. SITUATION.
    (a)   The enemy are retiring along the whole front of the Fourth Army.

    (b)   XIV Corps will advance their outpost line to-morrow on a line NERLU - MANANCOURT - LE MESNIL - ROCQUIGNY - BARASTRE with a view to making this line the main line of resistance at a date which will be notified later.

    (c)   XIV Corps cavalry are moving forward at 7 a.m. from LE MESNIL directed on EQUANCOURT and YTRES.

    (d)   2nd and 1st Guards Brigades will establish outposts on a general line V.27.b. - V.14.c. - U.12.central - U.5.central.

2. BOUNDARIES.
    Boundaries of 1st Guards Brigade will be as follows :-

    South U.16.central - U.18.c.5.0. - V.7.b.5.0.
    North U.3.a.7.3. - North edge of HAMMAR COPSE - North edge of LOON COPSE - MESNIL Church - U.5.a.9.5.

3.   2nd Bn. Grenadier Guards will continue to find the outpost line.

4.   The leading patrols will move from their present position at 8-30 a.m.

5. (a)   O.C., Outposts will establish a line of picquets on a line running approximately from U.5.a.6..7 - KOSCHAU TRENCH to U.5.c.7.1. - along line of Road running S.E. through U.11.b. - round Eastern edge of Copse in U.12.c. - Eastern edge of ST. MARTINS WOOD - U.18.central.

    (b)   He will establish posts on an approximate line U.5.a.9.7. - GALLWITZ Trench - BARTFIELD Trench U.6.c. and d. and U.12.b. - ETRICOURT Trench U.12.d. and V.7.c. to V.7.c.6.2. These posts will be consolidated as far as possible.

    (c)   He will establish a Support Line on an approximate line LE MESNIL Church - along Road running due South to BATOCKE Trench U.11.a.1.½. - BATOCKI Trench - TRESS Trench U.17.d. to U.17.d.5.1.

    (d)   He will select a suitable H.Q., in the vicinity of STAR Cross Roads U.10.c. and d. The position selected will be notified to Brigade H.Q., as soon as possible.

    (e)   The line of defence will be the Support Line.

6.   Communication will be kept with 2nd Guards Brigade on the Right (i.e. 1st Bn. Grenadier Guards) and 60th Brigade on the Left.

1.

2.

7. The four Machine Guns now allotted to O.C., Outposts will go forward with the Outposts. O.C., Bde. Machine Gun Company will reconnoitre positions and place his guns so that the flanks of the main line of defence are protected and the approaches to it covered.

H.Q., Machine Gun Company will move to U.13.b.9.4½.

8. Minor opposition will be dealt with but if opposition of more than a few hostile patrols is encountered no attack will be made without reference to Brigade H.Q.,

9. No Artillery will move forward in Support of the advance with the exception of one Section 20th Divnl. Artillery which has been detailed to move to about U.11.central with the object of supporting the Cavalry should the necessity arise.

10. 3rd Bn. Coldstream Guards will maintain it's present dispositions in Support. It's H.Q., will move to the HEBULE. To be clear of U.19.a.8.8. by 8-30 a.m.

11. An Advanced Brigade H.Q., will be established at U.19.a.8.8. at 8-30 a.m. to which place all messages will be sent after 8-30 a.m.

12. Administrative details will be communicated later by the Staff Captain.

ACKNOWLEDGE.

Captain,
Brigade Major, 1st Guards Brigade.

Issued through Signals at 3-45 A.M.

Copy No. 1 2nd Bn. Grenadier Guards.
2 2nd Bn. Coldstream Guards.
3 3rd Bn. Coldstream Guards.
4 1st Bn Irish Guards
5 Bde. Machine Gun Company.
6 Bde. Trench Mortar Bty.
7 Left Group, G.D.A.
8 Guards Division
9 2nd Guards Brigade.
10 3rd Guards Brigade.
11 60th Infantry Brigade.
12 75th Field Coy., R.E.
13 9th Field Ambulance.
14 Staff Captain.
15 O.C. Signals.
16 - 20 Retained.

SECRET.   Copy No. 18

App. 342

1st Guards Brigade Operation Order No.108.
****

18th March 1917.

1. SITUATION.

   (a)   1st Guards Brigade is holding a line BRUNSWICK Trench –
         POLE Trench – FERDINAND Trench with standing patrols in
         HAMMER Copse – BULGAR Trench – Cross Roads U 10 c and d central.

   (b)   1st Guards Brigade is in touch with 2nd Guards Brigade on
         the Right in BATOCKI Trench and at Cross Roads U 10 c and d
         and with 60th Brigade on the Left at the N.W. end of HAMMER
         Copse.

   (c)   The enemy are retiring rapidly on a line BUS – LECHELLE –
         EQUANCOURT. At present the exact line that he is holding is
         not known.

2.   2nd Bn. Grenadier Guards will relieve 3rd Bn. Coldstream
Guards in the outpost line to-night. O.C., 2nd Bn. Grenadier Guards
will be O.C., Outposts.

3.   Details and hour of relief will be arranged between C. O's.
concerned.

4.   O.C., Outposts will establish a line of picquets on an
approximate line HAMMER Copse – POLE Trench U 9 b 3.4. – FERDINAND
Trench between U 10 a 0.1. and U 10 c 2.3. – Quarry U 16 a 2.3.

        Groups will be established on an approximate line LOON Copse
– BULGAR Trench to the junction of BULGAR Trench and FERDINAND
Trench U 10 c 2.7½. – Cross Roads U 10 c and d thence Southwards
along the Road through U 16 a and c to U 16 a 4½.2½. A standing
patrol will be established at U 10 d 9.6. (junction of Road running
East from STAR Cross Roads with BATOCKI Trench).

        Support Line will be established on a line PLANET Trench –
BRUNSWICK Trench – GOTHA Trench – COBURG Trench.

        The line of defence will be the Support Line.

5.   The Brigade Boundaries will remain as before on the right
the line of the Railway running from U 15 d in an Easterly direction –
on the left a line running from the junction of PLANET and BRUNSWICK
Trenches, U 8 b 3.3. past the North Easterly edge of HAMMER Copse and
LOON Copse.

        Communication will be maintained with 2nd Guards Brigade
on the Right and 60th Brigade on the left.

6.   O.C., Outposts will arrange for active patrolling of LE MESNIL
– OPAKA Trench – AHCHISE Trench, but patrols will not proceed further
than 1,000 yards in an Easterly direction from the line of Groups.

7.   O.C., Outposts will arrange for systematic observation of
the high ground East of LE MESNIL.

2.

8. O.C., Outposts will establish his H.Q., in the vicinity of Road junction U 14 b 9½.8½., and will report which point he selected as H.Q.,

9. On relief 3rd Bn. Coldstream Guards will become the Battalion in Support. Their dispositions will be similar to those at present occupied by 2nd Bn. Grenadier Guards with the exception of Battalion H.Q., which will remain at U 19 a 8.8.

10. The positions of Brigade H.Q., and Other Units of the 1st Guards Brigade will remain as at present.

11. Administrative details will be communicated by the Staff Captain.

ACKNOWLEDGE.

[signature]
Captain,
Brigade Major, 1st Guards Brigade.

Issued through Signals at 3-15 p.m.

Copy No. 1 2nd Bn. Grenadier Guards.
2 2nd Bn. Coldstream Guards.
3 3rd Bn. Coldstream Guards.
4 1st Bn. Irish Guards.
5 Bde., Machine Gun Company.
6 Bde., Trench Mortar Battery.
7 Left Group, G.D.A.
8 Guards Division.
9 2nd Guards Brigade.
10 3rd Guards Brigade.
11 60th Infantry Brigade.
12 75th Field Coy., R.E.
13 9th Field Ambulance.
14 Staff Captain.
15 O.C., Signals.
16 - 20 Retained.

SECRET.   Copy No. 17

1st Guards Brigade Operation Order No. 109.
****
                                                    19th March 1917.

1. **SITUATION.**
   (a) The enemy are retiring along the whole front of the Fourth Army.

   (b) XIV Corps will advance their outpost line to-morrow on a line NERLU - MANANCOURT - LE MESNIL - ROCQUIGNY - BARASTRE with a view to making this line the main line of resistance at a date which will be notified later.

   (c) XIV Corps cavalry are moving forward at 7 a.m. from LE MESNIL directed on EQUANCOURT and YTRES.

   (d) 2nd and 1st Guards Brigades will establish outposts on a general line V.27.b. - V.14.c. - U.12.central - U.5.central.

2. **BOUNDARIES.**
   Boundaries of 1st Guards Brigade will be as follows :-

   South U.16.central - U.18.c.5.0. - V.7.b.5.0.
   North U.8.a.7.3. - North edge of HAMMAR COPSE - North edge of LOON COPSE - MESNIL Church - U.5.a.9.5.

3. 2nd Bn. Grenadier Guards will continue to find the outpost line.

4. The leading patrols will move from their present position at 8-30 a.m.

5. (a) O.C., Outposts will establish a line of picquets on a line running approximately from U.5.a.6..7 - KOSCHAU TRENCH to U.5.c.7.1. - along line of Road running S.E. through U.11.b. - round Eastern edge of Copse in U.12.c. - Eastern edge of ST. MARTINS WOOD - U.18.central.

   (b) He will establish posts on an approximate line U.5.a.9.7. - GALLWITZ Trench - BARTFIELD Trench U.6.c. and d. and U.12.b. - ETRICOURT Trench U.12.d. and V.7.c. to V.7.c.6.2. These posts will be consolidated as far as possible.

   (c) He will establish a Support Line on an approximate line LE MESNIL Church - along Road running due South to BATOCKE Trench U.11.a.1.½. - BATOCKI Trench - TRESS Trench U.17.d. to U.17.d.5.1.

   (d) He will select a suitable H.Q., in the vicinity of STAR Cross Roads U.10.c. and d. The position selected will be notified to Brigade H.Q., as soon as possible.

   (e) The line of defence will be the Support Line.

6. Communication will be kept with 2nd Guards Brigade on the Right (i.e. 1st Bn. Grenadier Guards) and 60th Brigade on the Left.

1.

2.

7. The four Machine Guns now allotted to O.C., Outposts will go forward with the Outposts. O.C., Bde. Machine Gun Company will reconnoitre positions and place his guns so that the flanks of the main line of defence are protected and the approaches to it covered.

H.Q., Machine Gun Company will move to U.13.b.9.4½.

8. Minor opposition will be dealt with but if opposition of more than a few hostile patrols is encountered no attack will be made without reference to Brigade H.Q.,

9. No Artillery will move forward in Support of the advance with the exception of one Section 20th Divnl. Artillery which has been detailed to move to about U.11.central with the object of supporting the Cavalry should the necessity arise.

10. 3rd Bn. Coldstream Guards will maintain it's present dispositions in Support. It's H.Q., will move to the HEBULE. To be clear of U.19.a.8.8. by 8-30 a.m.

11. An Advanced Brigade H.Q., will be established at U.19.a.8.8. at 8-30 a.m. to which place all messages will be sent after 8-30 a.m.

12. Administrative details will be communicated later by the Staff Captain.

ACKNOWLEDGE.

Captain,
Brigade Major, 1st Guards Brigade.

Issued through Signals at 3-45 A.M.

Copy No. 1 2nd Bn. Grenadier Guards.
2 2nd Bn. Coldstream Guards.
3 3rd Bn. Coldstream Guards.
4 1st Bn. Irish Guards.
5 Bde. Machine Gun Company.
6 Bde. Trench Mortar Bty.
7 Left Group, G.D.A.
8 Guards Division.
9 2nd Guards Brigade.
10 3rd Guards Brigade.
11 60th Infantry Brigade.
12 75th Field Coy., R.E.
13 9th Field Ambulance.
14 Staff Captain.
15 O.C. Signals.
16 - 20 Retained.

SECRET.   Copy No. 16

1st Guards Brigade Operation Order No. 110.

19th March 1917.

1. The 2nd Bn. Coldstream Guards will relieve 3rd Bn. Coldstream Guards in the Support Area and 1st Bn. Irish Guards will relieve 2nd Bn. Coldstream Guards in FREGICOURT - COMBLES Area during tomorrow, 20th inst.,

    Hours and details of relief will be arranged between C. O's. concerned.

    On relief 3rd Bn. Coldstream Guards will return to MAUREPAS Camp.

2. On completion of relief the dispositions of the 2nd Bn. Coldstream Guards and 1st Bn. Irish Guards will be as follows :-

    <u>2nd Bn. Coldstream Guards.</u>
    H.Q.,   HEBULE (U.9.c.5.2.)
    1 Company distributed in BETTYE Reserve BULLET Cross roads and GILBERT Trench
    1 Company in GREENHARD Trench.
    2 Companies distributed in depth in GOTHA Trench U.9.c.5.2. to the junction of COBURG Trench with the Railway (U.15.b. - BEYREUTH Trench U.15.a.1.9. to U.15.d.2.8.
    2 Lewis Gun Posts 1 Section strong in FERDINAND Trench at U.10.c.7.1. and U.10.c.2.9.

    <u>1st Bn. Irish Guards.</u>
    H.Q., FREGICOURT U.30.a.
    1 Company COMBLES.
    1 Company COMBLES Cemetery.
    1 Company HAIE WOOD.
    1 Company FREGICOURT.

3. Sapping Platoons of 1st Bn. Irish Guards will relieve Sapping Platoons of 3rd Bn. Coldstream Guards at MOUCHOIR COPSE.
    On completion of fatigues detailed for tomorrow 20th, Sapping Platoon of 3rd Bn. Coldstream Guards will rejoin it's Battalion in MAUREPAS Camp.

4. 2nd Bn. Grenadier Guards will continue to find the outposts.
    The line of Supports will remain the line of Defence.

    <u>ACKNOWLEDGE.</u>

                                                           Captain,
                                   <u>Brigade Major, 1st Guards Brigade.</u>
Issued through Signals at 8-30 p.m.

Copy.No.1 2nd Bn. Grenadier Gds.,   Copy No.7 Guards Division.
         2 2nd Bn. Coldstream Gds.   8 Loft Group, G.D.A.
         3 3rd Bn. Coldstream Gds.   9 3rd Guards Brigade.
         4 1st Bn. Irish Guards.   10 60th Infantry Brigade.
         5 Bde., Machine Gun Coy.,   11 75th Field Coy., R.E.
         6 Bde., Trench Mortar Bty.,   12 9th Field Ambulance.
                                             13 Staff Captain.
                                             14 O.C., Signals.
                                             15 - 19 Retained.

S E C R E T.   Copy No. 17

1st Guards Brigade Operation Order No. 110.

19th March 1917.

1. The 2nd Bn. Coldstream Guards will relieve 3rd Bn. Coldstream Guards in the Support Area and 1st Bn. Irish Guards will relieve 2nd Bn. Coldstream Guards in FREGICOURT – COMBLES Area during tomorrow, 20th inst.,

   Hours and details of relief will be arranged between C. O's. concerned.

   On relief 3rd Bn. Coldstream Guards will return to MAUREPAS Camp.

2. On completion of relief the dispositions of the 2nd Bn. Coldstream Guards and 1st Bn. Irish Guards will be as follows :-

   2nd Bn. Coldstream Guards.
   H.Q., HEBULE (U.9.c.5.2.)
   1 Company distributed in BETTYE Reserve BULLET Cross roads and GILBERT Trench.
   1 Company in GREENBARD Trench.
   2 Companies distributed in depth in GOTHA Trench U.9.c.5.2. to the junction of COBURG Trench with the Railway (U.15.b. - BEYREUTH Trench U 15 a.1.9. to U.15.d.2.8.
   2 Lewis Gun Posts 1 Section strong in FERDINAND Trench at U.10.c.7.1. and U.10.c.2.9.

   1st Bn. Irish Guards.
   H.Q., FREGICOURT U.30.a.
   1 Company COMBLES.
   1 Company COMBLES Cemetery.
   1 Company HAIE WOOD.
   1 Company FREGICOURT.

3. Sapping Platoon of 1st Bn. Irish Guards will relieve Sapping Platoon of 3rd Bn. Coldstream Guards at MOUCHOIR COPSE.
   On completion of fatigues detailed for tomorrow 20th, Sapping Platoon of 3rd Bn. Coldstream Guards will rejoin it's Battalion in MAUREPAS Camp.

4. 2nd Bn. Grenadier Guards will continue to find the outposts. The line of Supports will remain the line of Defence.

   ACKNOWLEDGE.

                                                      Captain,
                                   Brigade Major, 1st Guards Brigade.

Issued through Signals at 8-30 p.m.

Copy.No.1 2nd Bn. Grenadier Gds.,   Copy No.7 Guards Division.
       2 2nd Bn. Coldstream Gds.   8 Left Group, G.D.A.
       3 3rd Bn. Coldstream Gds.   9 3rd Guards Brigade.
       4 1st Bn. Irish Guards.   10 60th Infantry Brigade.
       5 Bde., Machine Gun Coy.,   11 75th Field Coy., R.E.
       6 Bde., Trench Mortar Bty.,   12 9th Field Ambulance.
                                            13 Staff Captain.
                                            14 O.C., Signals.
                                            15 - 19 Retained.

S E C R E T.   Copy No. 19

1st Guards Brigade Operation Order No. 111.

30th March 1917.

1. (a)   The 2nd Bn. Coldstream Guards will relieve the 2nd Bn. Grenadier Guards in the Outpost line tomorrow 21st inst.,

   (b)   On completion of relief O.C., 2nd Bn. Coldstream Guards will become O.C., Outposts.

   (c)   Details of relief will be arranged between C.O's. concerned.

2. BRIGADE BOUNDARIES.

   North - U.8.central - U.4.d.0.5. - along road to U.4.d.9.9. - U.4.b.7.3. - U.5.a.9.7. - O.35.d.5.0. throughout inclusive to Guards Division.

   South - U.16.central - U.18.c.5.0. - V.7.b.5.0.

3.   The main line of Defence and the Outpost line of resistance will remain as detailed in 1st G.B. No.36.

4.   Communication will be maintained with 3rd Guards Brigade on the Right and 60th Infantry Brigade on the Left.

5.   The relief of the Support line of the Outposts will not take place before 3 p.m.
      The relief of the Picquet and Group line will not take place before dusk, approximately 6 p.m.

6.   On relief the four Machine Guns now in position in the Outpost line will remain at the disposal of O.C., Outposts.

7. (a)   On relief 2nd Bn. Grenadier Guards will occupy the FREGICOURT - COMBLES Area with H.Q., at FREGICOURT Cross Roads.

   (b)   The 1st Bn. Irish Guards will take over the Area in Support from the 2nd Bn. Coldstream Guards with H.Q., and 2 Companies at HEBULE, 1 Company BULLET Cross Roads and BETTYE Reserve, 1 Kompany GREENHARD Trench.

          Details of relief will be made by C.O's concerned.

8.   The Sapping Platoon of 1st Bn. Irish Guards will relieve the Sapping Platoon of 2nd Bn. Grenadier Guards at MOUCHOIR Copse. On relief the Sapping Platoon of 2nd Bn. Grenadier Guards will rejoin it's Battalion.

9.   3rd Bn. Coldstream Guards will remain in it's present position.

10.   A Warning Order concerning the relief of the Division will be issued as soon as possible.

                ACKNOWLEDGE.   B Dyer Captain,
                                                    Brigade Major, 1st Guards Brigade.

No.1 2nd Bn.Gren.Gds.   No.6 T.M.Battery.   No.11 3rd Guards Brigade.
   2 2nd Bn. Coldstream Gds. No.7 Guards Div.   12 60th Infantry Bde.,
   3 3rd Bn. Cold.Gds.   8 Loft Group,G.D.A. 13 Supply Officer.
   4 1st Bn.Irish Gds.   9 75th FlsCoy.   14 Staff Captain.
   5 Bde.M.C.Coy.   10 9th Fld.Amb.   15 D.B.O.
                                                  16 O.C, Signals,
                                                  17 - 20 Retained.

SECRET.   Copy No. 18

AM 345

1st Guards Brigade Operation Order No. 111.

20th March 1917.

1. (a)   The 2nd Bn. Coldstream Guards will relieve the 2nd Bn.
            Grenadier Guards in the Outpost line tomorrow 21st inst.,

    (b)   On completion of relief O.C., 2nd Bn. Coldstream Guards
            will become O.C., Outposts.

    (c)   Details of relief will be arranged between C.O's. concerned.

2. BRIGADE BOUNDARIES.

    North - U.8.central - U.4.d.0.5. - along road to U.4.d.9.9. -
            U.4.b.7.3. - U.5.a.9.7. - O.35.d.5.0. throughout inclusive
            to Guards Division.

    South - U.16.central - U.18.c.5.0. - V.7.b.5.0.

3.   The main line of Defence and the Outpost line of resistance
    will remain as detailed in 1st G.B. No.36.

4.   Communication will be maintained with 3rd Guards Brigade on
    the Right and 60th Infantry Brigade on the Left.

5.   The relief of the Support line of the Outposts will not take place before
    3 p.m.
            The relief of the Picquet and Group line will not take place
    before dusk, approximately 6 p.m.

6.   On relief the four Machine Guns now in position in the
    Outpost line will remain at the disposal of O.C., Outposts.

7. (a)   On relief 2nd Bn. Grenadier Guards will occupy the
            FREGICOURT - COMBLES Area with H.Q., at FREGICOURT Cross Roads.

    (b)   The 1st Bn. Irish Guards will take over the Area in Support
            from the 2nd Bn. Coldstream Guards with H.Q., and 2 Companies
            at HEBULE, 1 Company BULLET Cross Roads and BETTYE Reserve,
            1 Company GREENHARD Trench.

            Details of relief will be made by C.O's concerned.

8.   The Sapping Platoon of 1st Bn. Irish Guards will relieve
    the Sapping Platoon of 2nd Bn. Grenadier Guards at MOUCHOIR Copse.
    On relief the Sapping Platoon of 2nd Bn. Grenadier Guards will
    rejoin it's Battalion.

9.   3rd Bn. Coldstream Guards will remain in it's present
    position.

10.   A Warning Order concerning the relief of the Division will
    be issued as soon as possible.

                                                        S. Dyer Captain,
            ACKNOWLEDGE.
                                            Brigade Major, 1st Guards Brigade.

    No.1 2nd Bn.Gren.Gds.   No.6 T.M.Battery.   No.11 3rd Guards Brigade.
       2 2nd Bn. Coldstream Gds. No.7 Guards Div.   12 60th Infantry Bde.,
       3 3rd Bn. Cold.Gds.   8 Loft Group,G.D.A. 13 Supply Officer.
       4 1st Bn.Irish Gds.   9 75th Fls.Coy.   14 Staff Captain.
       5 Bde.M.G.Coy.   10 9th Fld.Amb.   15 D.D.O.
                                                      16 O.C, Signals.
                                                      17 - 20 Retained.

SECRET.   Copy No. 19

AM 346

1st Guards Brigade Warning Order No. 112.

21st March 1917.

1. 1st Guards Brigade will be relieved by 20th Division in the front HANANCOURT (exclusive) - LE MESNIL, relief to be complete by 8 a.m. March 24th.

2. After relief the boundary between Guards Division and 20th Division will run as follows :- T.30.a.3.4. - U.19.b.8.8. - U.15.c.0.0. U.18.c.5.0. - V.7.d.0.0.

3. Guards Divnl. Artillery will remain supporting its present front.

4. Relief, details of which will be forwarded later, will take place as follows :-

Date.	Unit.	From.	To.
Mch. 22nd	3rd Bn. Cold. Gds.	MAUREPAS.	GUINCHY or MONTAUBAN.
	2nd Bn. Gren. Gds.	FREGICOURT.	" " "
	1st Bn. Irish Gds.	HESULE.	Outpost line.
	2nd Bn. Cold. Gds.	Outpost line.	HESULE.
23rd	2nd Bn. Cold. Gds.	HESULE.	MAUREPAS.
	1st Bn. Irish Gds.	Outpost line.	COMBLES.

5. Details of relief of Bde., Machine Gun Company and Trench Mortar Battery will be notified later.

ACKNOWLEDGE.

Captain,
Brigade Major, 1st Guards Brigade.

Copies to :-
No. 1 2nd Bn. Grenadier Guards.
 2 2nd Bn. Coldstream Guards.
 3 3rd Bn. Coldstream Guards.
 4 1st Bn. Irish Guards.
 5 Bde., Machine Gun Company.
 6 Bde., Trench Mortar Bty.,
 7 Guards Division.
 8 3rd Guards Brigade.
No. 9 2nd Guards Brigade.
 10 75th Field Coy., R.E.
 11 9th Field Ambulance.
 12 Supply Officer.
 13 Staff Captain.
 14 O.C., Signals.
 15 Bde., Bombing Officer.
 16 - 20 Retained.

SECRET.   1st G.S. No. 36.

2nd Bn. Grenadier Guards.
2nd Bn. Coldstream Guards.
3rd Bn. Coldstream Guards.
1st Bn. Irish Guards.
Bde., Machine Gun Company.
Bde., Trench Mortar Battery.

1. There has been some confusion between the line of resistance (of the <u>Outposts</u>) and the main line of Defence (of the <u>Division</u>).

2. In the event of attack the Outposts will defend their line of resistance (in this case the <u>Picquet line</u>) as long as possible in order to give time for the main line of Defence of the Division to be occupied by the main body.

3. The main line of Defence (U.10.a.8.9. - BULGAR Trench - U.10.central - Star Cross Roads - U.16.central) will be occupied at once by Machine Guns placed in position by O.C., Machine Gun Company.
The exact co-ordinates of where these Guns are placed will be notified later.

4. The line of the Picquets (line of resistance of outposts) is now approximately as follows :- U.5.a.6.8½. - KASCHAU Trench to U.5.c.6.5. - U.12.a.5.0. ETRICOURT Trench U.12.c.8.8. to V.7.c.7.2.
This alteration is in consequence of the 3rd Guards Brigade having advanced their line on our Right.

5. The Support line of the Outposts will be advanced approximately as follows :- U.4.b.7.5. - along Dunk Road U.5.c. - U.11.a. - U.11.c. U.11.d. to U.18.central.

Captain,

20th March 1917.   Brigade Major, 1st Guards Brigade.

SECRET.   Copy No. 17

1st Guards Brigade Warning Order No. 112.

21st March 1917.

1. 1st Guards Brigade will be relieved by 20th Division in the front HANANCOURT (exclusive) - LE MESNIL, relief to be complete by 8 a.m. March 24th.

2. After relief the boundary between Guards Division and 20th Division will run as follows :- T.30.a.3.4. - U.19.b.8.8. - U.15.c.0.0. U.18.c.5.0. - V.7.d.0.0.

3. Guards Divnl. Artillery will remain supporting its present front.

4. Relief, details of which will be forwarded later, will take place as follows :-

Date.	Unit.	From.	To.
Mch. 22nd	3rd Bn. Cold. Gds.	MAUREPAS.	GUINCHY or MONTAUBAN.
	2nd Bn. Gren. Gds.	FREGICOURT.	" " "
	1st Bn. Irish Gds.	HEBULE.	Outpost line.
	2nd Bn. Cold. Gds.	Outpost line.	HEBULE.
23rd	2nd Bn. Cold. Gds.	HEBULE.	MAUREPAS.
	1st Bn. Irish Gds.	Outpost line.	COMBLES.

5. Details of relief of Bde., Machine Gun Company and Trench Mortar Battery will be notified later.

ACKNOWLEDGE.

Captain,
Brigade Major, 1st Guards Brigade.

Copies to :-
  No. 1 2nd Bn. Grenadier Guards.   No. 9 2nd Guards Brigade.
     2   2nd Bn. Coldstream Guards.   10 75th Field Coy., R.E.
     3   3rd Bn. Coldstream Guards.   11 9th Field Ambulance.
     4   1st Bn. Irish Guards.   12 Supply Officer.
     5   Bde., Machine Gun Company.   13 Staff Captain.
     6   Bde., Trench Mortar Bty.,   14 O.C., Signals.
     7   Guards Division.   15 Bde., Bombing Officer.
     8   3rd Guards Brigade.   16 - 20 Retained.

60th Inf. Bde. 21

SECRET.   Copy No. 20
=======   ============

                    App 347

                1st Guards Brigade Operation Order No. 113.
                ⁕=⁕=⁕=⁕=⁕=⁕=⁕=⁕=⁕=⁕=⁕=⁕=⁕=⁕=⁕=⁕=⁕

                                                            21st March 1917.

1.   1st Bn. Irish Guards will relieve 2nd Bn. Coldstream Guards
in the Outpost line tomorrow, 22nd inst.,

        On relief O.C., 1st Bn. Irish Guards will be O.C., Outposts.
2nd Bn. Coldstream Guards will be in Support in the HEMULE Area.
        Details of relief will be arranged between C.O's. concerned.

        The relief of the Support Line of the Outposts will not take
2. place before 3 p.m, The relief of the Picquet and Group Lines will
    not take place before dusk, approximately 6 p.m

3. (a) Divisional Boundaries and the line of resistance of the Picquets
        remain unaltered.

    (b) The main line of Defence of the Division will be approximately
        as follows :- KASCHAU Trench U.5.a.6.5. - Star Cross Roads
        U.10.c. and d. - U.16 central.

4.   Communication will be maintained with 3rd Guards Brigade on
the Right and 60th Infantry Brigade on the Left.

5. (a) The four Machine Guns in position in the Outpost line will
        come under the Orders of O.C., Outposts on completion of the
        relief.

    (b) Eight Machine Guns are now in positions detailed below
        protecting the main line of Defence as detailed before the
        alteration in para.3 (b). was notified. The adjustments
        necessary to conform to the new line will be made early
        tomorrow, 22nd inst.,
        The positions occupied by M.G's at present:-
                    No.2 Gun U.16.b.2.1½.
                       3 " U.16.b.3.2½.
                       4 " U.16.b.2½.6.
                       5 " U.10.d.3.9.
                       6 " U.10.a.8½.2.
                       7 " U.10.a.7.4¾.
                       8 " U.11.c.2½.1.

        No. 1 Gun at U.16.b.2.8. has been taken over by 3rd Guards Bde.,

6.   2nd Bn. Grenadier Guards will move tomorrow, 22nd inst., from
FREGICOURT - HAIE WOOD - COMBLES Area to GINCHY T.19.a.0.5. where
they will take over billets vacated by 20th Division Works Battn.,
        These billets will be vacated by 20th Division Works Battn.,
by 2 p.m.
        The FREGICOURT - HAIE WOOD - COMBLES Area will be vacated by
2nd Bn. Grenadier Guards by 2 p.m.
        60th Infantry Brigade is arranging to send caretakers to
report to H.Q., 2nd Bn. Grenadier Guards FREGICOURT by 10 a.m.
to take over the FREGICOURT - HAIE WOOD - COMBLES Area, which will
not be occupied by Units of the 20th Division until the 23rd inst.,

7.   3rd Bn. Coldstream Guards, Bde., Machine Gun Company and Trench
Mortar Battery will remain in their present positions on 22nd inst.,

(2)

8.   On 23rd inst., movements will take place according to the attached Table (Appendix "A".)
       Details will be communicated later.

9.   Details of Working Parties on completion of relief by 60th Infantry Brigade are shown in Appendix "B".

10.   Positions of Units on March 24th are shown in Appendix "C".

ACKNOWLEDGE.

J.S.Dyer
Captain,
Brigade Major, 1st Guards Brigade.

Issued through Signals at 10 p.m.

Copy No.1 2nd Bn. Grenadier Guards.
     2 2nd Bn. Coldstream Guards.
     3 3rd Bn. Coldstream Guards.
     4 1st Bn. Irish Guards.
     5 Bde., Machine Gun Company.
     6 Bde., Machine Gun Company.
     7 Guards Division.
     8 3rd Guards Brigade.
     9 2nd Guards Brigade.
    10 60th Infantry Brigade.
    11 75th Field Coy., R.E.
    12 9th Field Ambulance.
    13 Supply Officer.
    14 Staff Captain.
    15 Signals.
    16 B.B.O.
    17 - 21 Retained.

APPENDIX "A".
****

Unit.	From.	To.	Relieving.	Relieved by.
1/Irish Gds.	Outpost Line.	COMBLES.	1/Scots Gds.	12th K.R.R. 12th R.B.
2/Cold Gds	HEBULE.	MAUREPAS.	1/Gren Gds.	*
3/Cold Gds.	MAUREPAS.	MONTAUBAN.	20th Divn, Works Bn.,	*
Bde M G Coy.	Line.	MAUREPAS.	*	Bde.M.G.Coy. 60th Bde.
Bde.T.M.Bty.	HAIE WOOD.	MAUREPAS.	*	Bde.T.M.Bty. 60th Bde.,
Brigade H.Q., U.9.a.U.8.		BOIS DOUAGE.		

* = To be notified later.

APPENDIX "B".

Unit.	At.	Work.		
2/Grenadier Gds.	GUINCHY. I.19.a.0.5. LES BOEUFS & LE TRANSLOY Rd.	Will receive Orders from. C.E. XIV Corps.	Begin work on March - 23rd.
2/Coldstream Gds.	MAUREPAS.	Roads.	Corps Roads Officer.	24th.
3/Coldstream Gds.	MONTAUBAN.	2 Coy's. LES BOEUFS LE TRANSLOY Rd. 2 Coys. Broadgauge Railway.	C.E. XIV Corps. 295th Rly. Coy. R.E.	24th.
1/Irish Gds.	COMBLES.	Road COMBLES — FREGICOURT — SAILLY SAILLISEL - O.31.d.3.9.	C.R.E. Guards Divn.	25th.

APPENDIX "C".

Unit.	At.
2/Grenadier Gds.	GUINCHY T.19.a.0.5.
2/Coldstream Gds.	MAUREPAS.
3/Coldstream Gds.	MONTAUBAN.
1/Irish Gds.	COMBLES.
Bde.M.G.Company.	MAUREPAS.
Bde.T.M.Battery.	MAUREPAS.
Brigade H.Q.,	BOIS DOUAGE.

S E C R E T.　　　　　　　　　　　　　　　　　　　　　Copy No. 19

1st Guards Brigade Operation Order No. 113.

21st March 1917.

1. 1st Bn. Irish Guards will relieve 2nd Bn. Coldstream Guards in the Outpost line tomorrow, 22nd inst.,

    On relief O.C., 1st Bn. Irish Guards will be O.C., Outposts. 2nd Bn. Coldstream Guards will be in Support in the HECULE Area. Details of relief will be arranged between C.O's. concerned.

2. The relief of the Support Line of the Outposts will not take place before 3 p.m. The relief of the Picquet and Group Lines will not take place before dusk, approximately 6 p.m.

3. (a) Divisional Boundaries and the line of resistance of the Picquets remain unaltered.

    (b) The main line of Defence of the Division will be approximately as follows :- KASCHAU Trench J.5.a.6.5. - Star Cross Roads U.10.c. and d. - U 16 central.

4. Communication will be maintained with 3rd Guards Brigade on the Right and 60th Infantry Brigade on the Left.

5. (a) The four Machine Guns in position in the Outpost line will come under the Orders of O.C., Outposts on completion of the relief.

    (b) Eight Machine Guns are now in positions detailed below protecting the main line of Defence as detailed before the alteration in para 3 (b). was notified. The adjustments necessary to conform to the new line will be made early tomorrow, 22nd inst., *The positions occupied by M.G's at present are:-*

    No. 2 Gun U.16.b.2.1½.
    　3　"　U.16.b.3.2½.
    　4　"　U.16.b.2½.6.
    　5　"　U.10.d.3.8.
    　6　"　U.10.a.8½.2.
    　7　"　U.10.a.7.4¾.
    　8　"　U.11.c.2½.1.

    No. 1 Gun at U.16.b.2.8. has been taken over by 3rd Guards Bde.,

6. 2nd Bn. Grenadier Guards will move tomorrow, 22nd inst., from FREGICOURT - HAIE WOOD - COMBLES Area to GINCHY T.19.a.0.5. where they will take over billets vacated by 20th Division Works Battn.,
    These billets will be vacated by 20th Division Works Battn., by 2 p.m.
    The FREGICOURT - HAIE WOOD - COMBLES Area will be vacated by 2nd Bn. Grenadier Guards by 2 p.m.
    60th Infantry Brigade is arranging to send caretakers to report to H.Q., 2nd Bn. Grenadier Guards FREGICOURT by 10 a.m. to take over the FREGICOURT - HAIE WOOD - COMBLES Area, which will not be occupied by Units of the 20th Division until the 23rd inst.,

7. 3rd Bn. Coldstream Guards, Bde., Machine Gun Company and Trench Mortar Battery will remain in their present positions on 22nd inst.,

(2)

8. On 23rd inst., movements will take place according to the attached Table (Appendix "A".)
   Details will be communicated later.

9. Details of Working Parties on completion of relief by 60th Infantry Brigade are shown in Appendix "B".

10. Positions of Units on March 24th are shown in Appendix "C".

    ACKNOWLEDGE.

    J.S.Dyer
    Captain,
    Brigade Major, 1st Guards Brigade.

Issued through Signals at 10 p.m.

Copy No. 1 2nd Bn. Grenadier Guards.
     2 2nd Bn. Coldstream Guards.
     3 3rd Bn. Coldstream Guards.
     4 1st Bn. Irish Guards.
     5 Bde., Machine Gun Company.
     6 Bde., Machine Gun Company.
     7 Guards Division.
     8 3rd Guards Brigade.
     9 2nd Guards Brigade.
    10 60th Infantry Brigade.
    11 75th Field Coy., R.E.
    12 9th Field Ambulance.
    13 Supply Officer.
    14 Staff Captain.
    15 Signals.
    16 B.S.O.
    17 - 21 Retained.

APPENDIX "A".
****

Unit.	From.	To.	Relieving.	Relieved by.
1/Irish Gds.	Outpost Line.	COMBLES.	1/Scots Gds.	12th K.R.R. 12th R.B.
2/Cold.Gds.	HEDULE.	MAUREPAS.	1/Gren Gds.	*
3/Cold.Gds.	MAUREPAS.	MONTAUBAN.	20th Divn. Works Bn.	*
Bde M G Coy.	Line.	MAUREPAS.	*	Bde.M.G.Coy. 60th Bde.
Bde.T.M.Bty.	HAIE WOOD.	MAUREPAS.	*	Bde.T.M.Bty. 60th Bde.
Brigade H.Q., U.9.a.8.8.		BOIS DOUAGE.		

* = To be notified later.

APPENDIX "B".
****

Unit.	At.	Work.	Will receive Orders from.	Begin work on March -
2/Grenadier Gds.	GUINCHY. T.19.a.0.5.	LES BOEUFS & LE TRANSLOY Rd.	C.E. XIV Corps.	23rd.
2/Coldstream Gds.	MAUREPAS.	Roads.	Corps Roads Officer.	24th.
3/Coldstream Gds.	MONTAUBAN.	2 Coy's. LES BOEUFS LE TRANSLOY Rd. 2 Coys. Broadgauge Railway.	C.E. XIV Corps. 295th Rly. Coy. R.E.	24th.
1/Irish Gds.	COMBLES.	Road COMBLES - FREGICOURT - SAILLY SAILLISEL - O.31.d.3.9.	C.R.E. Guards Divn.	25th.

APPENDIX "C".
****

Unit.	At.
2/Grenadier Gds.	GUINCHY T.19.a.0.5.
2/Coldstream Gds.	MAUREPAS.
3/Coldstream Gds.	MONTAUBAN.
1/Irish Gds.	COMBLES.
Bde. M.G. Company. Bde. T.M. Battery.	MAUREPAS.
Brigade H.Q.,	BOIS DOUAGE.

SECRET.   Copy No. 11

1st Guards Brigade Order No 114.

APP 348

22nd March 1917.

1.   O.C. 2nd Bn Coldstream Guards will arrange to occupy the main line of defence with one Company as soon as possible tomorrow 23rd inst. This Company will occupy a line running approximately U 11 a 1.2 - between the German wire covering OPAKA Trench-U 16 b 6.9 - sunk road U 16 b 2.5.

The garrison of the main line of defence will then be one Company of the reserve Battalion and 7 machine guns, the exact positions of which will be notified later.

2.   O.C. 2nd Bn Coldstream Guards will make arrangements at once to dig trenches on this line and construct wire entanglements to protect it.

As much use as possible should be made of the German wire already in existence.

3.   The line of picquets (i.e. line of resistance of the Outposts) will be wired without delay.

Wire is obtainable from the Dumps at MUTZ Copse, and at the end of the Railway U 16 M. There are also large quantities of wire already in existing entanglements and lying about in coils all over the Country.

ACKNOWLEDGE.

Captain.

Brigade Major, 1st Guards Bde.

Copy No 1.   2nd Bn Grenadier Guards.
        2.   2nd Bn Coldstream Guards.
        3.   3rd Bn Coldstream Guards.
        4.   1st Bn Irish Guards.
        5.   Bde. Machine Gun Coy.
        6.   Bde. T.M.Battery.
        7.   Guards Division.
        8.   3rd Guards Brigade.
        9.   60th Inf. Bde.
        10. Left Group, R.G.A.
        11 & 12 Retained.

SECRET.   1st G.B. No. 59.

2nd Bn. Grenadier Guards.   Bde., Trench Mortar Battery.
2nd Bn. Coldstream Guards.   3rd Guards Brigade.
3rd Bn. Coldstream Guards.   60th Infantry Brigade.
1st Bn. Irish Guards.   Left Group, G.D.A.
Bde. Machine Gun Company.

1.   On receipt of orders from Brigade H.Q., 2nd Bn. Coldstream Guards in Support, and 1 Section Machine Gun Company ub Reserve in SAILLY SAILLISEL, will be prepared at once to reinforce the main Line of Defence (KASCHAU TRENCH - STAR Cross Roads - U.16.central).

2.   Coy's. and Machine Guns will be told off in advance to their respective positions in the main Line of Defence to which they would be sent forward.
        Officers concerned will be acquainted with the routes leading to their respective positions.

3.   In the event of a hostile attack on the Outpost Line of resistance (i.e. the Picquet Line).

   (a) The Outposts, 1st Bn. Irish Guards, will defend the Outpost line of resistance as long as possible. If forced to fall back they will reform in the next suitable position giving up as little ground as possible to the enemy.

   (b) The main Line of Defence will be reinforced from the Supporting Battalion (2nd Bn. Coldstream Guards).

   (c) Brigade H.Q., will keep the Artillery informed of the position of the leading troops so that Artillery Support can be afforded if and when the Outpost troops are forced back sufficiently far for our Guns to shoot beyond them.

4.   The deep dugout in U.9.b.2.4. (POLE Trench) will be the Command Post to which O.C., Supporting Battalion would go in the event of him being called on to reinforce the main Line of Defence.

5.   In view of the fact that the present Line of resistance will, within 10 days, become the main Line of Defence every effort must be made to wire the Picquet Line (vide 1st Guards Brigade Order No.114. para.3.)
        Arrangements will also be made to barricade all roads leading into the position. This can be done temporarily by "Knife rests" which are already available and eventually by old wagons timber etc.,

22nd March 1917.   Brigade Major, 1st Guards Brigade.
                                                                 Captain.

SECRET.   App. 350   Copy No. 20

1st Guards Brigade Operation Order No. 115.

22nd March 1917.

1. 1st Bn. Irish Guards will be relieved by Units of the 60th Infantry Brigade in the Outpost Line tomorrow 23rd inst., relief to be completed by 8 a.m. 24th inst.,

    (a) The left Outpost Company will be relieved by 12th R.B.

    (b) The remaining three Outpost Coy's. will be relieved by 12th K.R.R.

    (c) Battn., H.Q., 1st Bn. Irish Guards will be relieved by Battn., H.Q., 12th K.R.R.

    (d) Details of the relief with the exception of Guides will be arranged by O.O's. concerned.

    (e) 1 Guide per Platoon will be at Star Cross Roads at 3 p.m.

    (f) On completion of relief 1st Bn. Irish Guards will take over billets in COMBLES T.28.c. vacated by 1st Bn. Scots Gds.,

    (g) Billeting parties will report to H.Q., 1st Bn. Scots Guards by 10 a.m.

2. Boundary between Guards Division and 20th Division after relief will be T.30.a.5.4. - U.19.b.8.8. - U.15.c.0.0. - U.18.c.5.0. - V.7.d.0.0.

3. 1st Guards Bde. Machine Gun Company will be relieved by 60th Infantry Bde. Machine Gun Company, tomorrow, 23rd inst.,

    (a) The four Machine Guns now at the disposal of O.C., Outposts will be relieved by 4 Machine Guns of the 60th Infantry Bde. Machine Gun Company.
    O.C., Outposts will arrange for one Guide for each Gun to be at Star Cross Roads. These Guides should not be taken from the Machine Gun Teams. O.C., Outposts will notify O.C., Bde. Machine Gun Company when these Guns have been relieved.

    (b) The seven Machine Guns now in position on the main Line of Defence will be relieved by 4 Machine Guns of the 60th Bde. Machine Gun Company.
    O.C., 1st Guards Bde. Machine Gun Company will arrange with O.C., 60th Infantry Bde. Machine Gun Company which Gun positions will be taken over and detail 1 Guide (4 in all) for each Gun concerned to be at Star Cross Roads at 3 p.m.
    On completion of the relief of these 4 Machine Guns O.C., Machine Gun Company will withdraw the remaining 3 Guns.

    (c) O.C., Bde., Machine Gun Company will send billeting parties to report to the Town Major, MAUREPAS, at 10 a.m.

4. The 2nd Bn. Coldstream Guards will be relieved by 6th Bn., Ox & Bucks in Support.

    (a) The dispositions of the 6th Ox & Bucks will be as follows :-
    Battn. H.Q., U.14.c.2.9½. 2 Coy's. BULLET Cross Roads, BETTYE Reserve and SOUTH Copse. 1 Company in main Line of Defence, approximately U.11.a.1.2. behind German wire covering OPAKA Trench U.16.b.5.9. to Sunk Road U.16.b.2.5. 1 Company LOON Copse (accommodation to be taken over from 12th R.B.)

1.

(b) O.C., 2nd Bn. Coldstream Guards will arrange to have 1 Guide per Platoon for the Company which will occupy the main Line of Defence at U.14.c.2.9½. at 3 p.m.

(c) Details of the relief of the other two Coy's. which will relieve 2nd Bn. Coldstream Guards will be arranged between O.C's. concerned.

(d) O.C., 6th Ox & Bucks will inform O.C., 2nd Bn. Coldstream Guards as soon as his Coy's. have taken up the positions outlined above.

(5) (a) The 6th K.S.L.I. will take over the Reserve Battn., Area and will be disposed as follows :- Battn., H.Q., and 6 Platoons at FREGICOURT, two Platoons MOUCHOIR Copse, two Coy's. HEDULE. No Guides are required.

(b) O.C., 6th K.S.L.I. will inform O.C., 2nd Bn. Coldstream Guards as soon as the 2 Coy's. at the HEDULE are in position.

(c) On completion of relief 2nd Bn. Coldstream Guards will take over billets from 1st Bn. Grenadier Guards in MAUREPAS Camp.

(d) Billeting parties will report to H.Q., 1st Bn. Grenadier Guards at 10 a.m.

6. Sapping Platoons of 2nd Bn. Coldstream Guards and 1st Bn. Irish Guards will, on relief by 2 Platoons 6th K.S.L.I., rejoin their Battn's. at MAUREPAS and COMBLES respectively.

7. (a) 3rd Bn. Coldstream Guards will take over billets at MONTAUBAN vacated by 20th Divn. Works Battn., tomorrow, 23rd inst

(b) Billets now occupied at MAUREPAS will be vacated by 2 p.m.

(c) Billeting parties will report to the Town Major, MONTAUBAN, at 10 a.m.

8. O.C., 60th Trench Mortar Battery will inform O.C., 1st Guards Bde Trench Mortar Battery in HAIE WOOD when he has moved into dugouts in T.17.d. 1st Guards Bde. Trench Mortar Battery will then move to MAUREPAS Billeting party will report to Town Major, MAUREPAS, by 10 a.m.

9. Administrative arrangements, positions of Transport Lines, etc., will be notified by Staff Captain.

10. 1st Guards Bde., H.Q., will close at U.10.a.8.8. at 3 p.m. and open at BOIS DOUAGE at the same hour.

ACKNOWLEDGE.

J.S. Dyer.
Captain,
Brigade Major, 1st Guards Brigade.

Issued through Signals at 8-30 a.m.
Copy No. 1 2nd Bn. Grenadier Gds.   Copy No.10 60th Infantry Brigade.
        2 2nd Bn. Coldstream Gds.   11 Loft Group, G.D.A.
        3 3rd Bn. Coldstream Gds.   12 75th Field Coy. R.E.
        4 1st Bn. Irish Gds.   13 9th Field Ambulance.
        5 Bde. Machine Gun Company.   14 Supply Officer.
        6 Bde. Trench Mortar Battery.   15 Staff Captain.
        7 Guards Division.   16 Bde. Bombing Officer.
        8 3rd Guards Brigade.   17 O.C., Signals.
        9 2nd Guards Brigade.   18 - 21 Retained.

SECRET.   Copy No. 19

1st Guards Brigade Operation Order No. 115.

22nd March 1917.

1.   1st Bn. Irish Guards will be relieved by Units of the 60th Infantry Brigade in the Outpost Line tomorrow 23rd inst., relief to be completed by 6 a.m. 24th inst.,

   (a)   The left Outpost Company will be relieved by 12th R.B.

   (b)   The remaining three Outpost Coy's. will be relieved by 12th K.R.R.

   (c)   Battn., H.Q., 1st Bn. Irish Guards will be relieved by Battn., H.Q., 12th K.R.R.

   (d)   Details of the relief with the exception of Guides will be arranged by O.O's. concerned.

   (e)   1 Guide per Platoon will be at Star Cross Roads at 3 p.m.

   (f)   On completion of relief 1st Bn. Irish Guards will take over billets in COMBLES T.28.c. vacated by 1st Bn. Scots Gds.,

   (g)   Billeting parties will report to H.Q., 1st Bn. Scots Guards by 10 a.m.

2.   Boundary between Guards Division and 20th Division after relief will be T.30.a.5.4. - U.19.b.8.8. - U.15.c.0.0. - U.18.c.5.0. - V.7.d.0.0.

3.   1st Guards Bde. Machine Gun Company will be relieved by 60th Infantry Bde. Machine Gun Company, tomorrow, 23rd inst.,

   (a)   The four Machine Guns now at the disposal of O.C., Outposts will be relieved by 4 Machine Guns of the 60th Infantry Bde. Machine Gun Company.
   O.C., Outposts will arrange for one Guide for each Gun to be at Star Cross Roads. These Guides should not be taken from the Machine Gun Teams. O.C., Outposts will notify O.C., Bde. Machine Gun Company when these Guns have been relieved.

   (b)   The seven Machine Guns now in position on the main Line of Defence will be relieved by 4 Machine Guns of the 60th Bde. Machine Gun Company.
   O.C., 1st Guards Bde. Machine Gun Company will arrange with O.C., 60th Infantry Bde. Machine Gun Company which Gun positions will be taken over and detail 1 Guide (4 in all) for each Gun concerned to be at Star Cross Roads at 3 p.m.
   On completion of the relief of these 4 Machine Guns O.C., Machine Gun Company will withdraw the remaining 3 Guns.

   (c)   O.C., Bde., Machine Gun Company will send billeting parties to report to the Town Major, MAUREPAS, at 10 a.m.

4.   The 2nd Bn. Coldstream Guards will be relieved by 6th Bn., Ox & Bucks in Support.

   (a)   The dispositions of the 6th Ox & Bucks will be as follows :-
   Battn. H.Q., U.14.c.2.9½. 2 Coy's. BULLET Cross Roads, BETTYE Reserve and SOUTH Copse. 1 Company in main Line of Defence, approximately U.11.a.1.2. behind German wire covering OPAKK Trench U.16.b.5.9. to Sunk Road U.16.b.2.5. 1 Company LOON Copse (accommodation to be taken over from 12th R.B.)

2.

(b) O.C., 2nd Bn. Coldstream Guards will arrange to have 1 Guide per Platoon for the Company which will occupy the main Line of Defence at U.14.c.2.9½. at 3 p.m.

(c) Details of the relief of the other two Coy's. which will relieve 2nd Bn. Coldstream Guards will be arranged between C.O's. concerned.

(d) O.C., 6th Ox & Bucks will inform O.C., 2nd Bn. Coldstream Guards as soon as his Coy's. have taken up the positions outlined above.

(5) (a) The 6th K.S.L.I. will take over the Reserve Battn., Area and will be d~~ disposed as follows :- Battn., H.Q., and 6 Platoons at FREGICOURT, two Platoons MOUCHOIR Copse, two Coy's. HEBULE. No Guides are required.

(b) O.C., 6th K.S.L.I. will inform O.C., 2nd Bn. Coldstream Guards as soon as the 2 Coy's. at the HEBULE are in position.

(c) On completion of relief 2nd Bn. Coldstream Guards will take over billets from 1st Bn. Grenadier Guards in MAUREPAS Camp.

(d) Billeting parties will report to H.Q., 1st Bn. Grenadier Guards at 10 a.m.

6. Sapping Platoons of 2nd Bn. Coldstream Guards and 1st Bn. Irish Guards will, on relief by 2 Platoons 6th K.S.L.I., rejoin their Battn's. at MAUREPAS and COMBLES respectively.

7. (a) 3rd Bn. Coldstream Guards will take over billets at MONTAUBAN vacated by 20th Divn. Works Battn., tomorrow, 23rd inst

(b) Billets now occupied at MAUREPAS will be vacated by 2 p.m.

(c) Billeting parties will report to the Town Major, MONTAUBAN, at 10 a.m.

8. O.C., 60th Trench Mortar Battery will inform O.C., 1st Guards Bde Trench Mortar Battery in HAIE WOOD when he has moved into dugouts in T.17.d. 1st Guards Bde. Trench Mortar Battery will then move to MAUREPAS Billeting party will report to Town Major, MAUREPAS, by 10 a.m.

9. Administrative arrangements, positions of Transport Lines, etc., will be notified by Staff Captain.

10. 1st Guards Bde., H.Q., will close at U.10.a.8.8. at 3 p.m. and open at BOIS DOUAGE at the same hour.

ACKNOWLEDGE.

J.S. Dyer.
Captain,
Brigade Major, 1st Guards Brigade.

Issued through Signals at 8-30 a.m.
Copy No.1 2nd Bn. Grenadier Gds.   Copy No.10 60th Infantry Brigade.
        2 2nd Bn. Coldstream Gds.   11 Left Group, G.D.A.
        3 3rd Bn. Coldstream Gds.   12 75th Field Coy. R.E.
        4 1st Bn. Irish Gds.   13 9th Field Ambulance.
        5 Bde. Machine Gun Company.   14 Supply Officer.
        6 Bde. Trench Mortar Battery.   15 Staff Captain.
        7 Guards Division.   16 Bde. Bombing Officer.
        8 3rd Guards Brigade.   17 O.C., Signals.
        9 2nd Guards Brigade.   18 - 21 Retained.

NOTES ON A CONFERENCE HELD AT BRIGADE H.Q.,

30th March 1917.

TRAINING.
1.
The Brigadier read through the proposed scheme for training to be carried out by this Brigade when the Division goes back into the Training Area.
It was essential that Commanding Officers should begin at once in the training of Officers and N.C.O's, and whenever possible those men of the Battalion who from time to time available.

(a) Bayonet Fighting. Inter-platoon bayonet fighting Competitions were to be considered an order. Commanding Officers should get their Pioneers to construct courses and would be helped in this matter by the Instructors.

(b) Musketry. Great care was to be taken in Musketry Instruction to get the highest standard possible from the men. Before firing on the range each individual man's faults should be carefully checked. On the range Instructors should remember to watch the man, and check him when necessary, instead of looking at the target.

(c) In all training great stress must be laid on the importance of properly studying the ground. During trench warfare this was very apt to be given only slight attention. It should be borne in mind that it is not necessary to always have a continuous trench, provided that all the ground is covered by fire.

(d) Sunday. On Sundays there would be no training, but Church parades should be made an opportunity for a smart turn-out.

The Brigadier wishes it impressed on all ranks that the withdrawal of the Division from the line did not mean a rest but a period for training and hard training at that. A good day's work should always be put in. It was most important that on the Division returning to the line it should be as efficient as possible, this could only be achieved by hard work.

The Brigadier then dealt with points arising from the Divisional Conference.

SUBORDINATE
COMMANDERS.
2.
Every Officer Commanding a Unit should have in case of need a fully qualified substitute to succeed him. Attention should be paid to training of Subordinate Commanders with this in view.

OFFICERS KIT.
3.
Every Officer should draw a man's jacket which could be altered by Master Tailors so as to fit properly. This jacket would only be used when actually going into an attack. Officers could wear knicker-bockers but might not carry sticks.

BLANK.
4.
Men should never be allowed to have blank and live ammunition in their possession at the same time. Special care should be taken too, when using dummy ammunition.

DRESS.
5.
Dress for training will always be Fighting Orders

WIRE CUTTING REPORT.
6.
The specimen copy of this report was explained and approved.

SAPPING PLATOONS.
7. When the Division goes back to train, men composing these Units will return to their ~~Battalions~~ *Platoons* and be trained like everyone else.

They will be re-assembled only if wanted for a particular task or when the Division returns to the Line.

RECOMMENDATIONS.
8. Care should be taken that only really genuine cases should be sent forward and that they should be put as strongly as possible.

COOKING.
9. If men did not eat all their rations less was to be drawn. In all cases full value should be got out of rations drawn. Bones, Scraps, etc., should be utilised.

WAGGONS.
10. The Major-General has made a ruling that the men attached to A.S.C., Units should do their turn as Guard over their waggons when necessary, and that they should be detailed by N.C.O's of the A.S.C.,

Appendix VI K.R. could not be quoted as Active Service.

When Battalions move and require Waggons, they should not demand them direct from the A.S.C., but through the usual channels. The Division would if necessary take waggons off other duties to provide the numbers asked for.

BAYONET FIGHTING. *Divisional*
11. A new Course is to be started at BRONFAY CAMP for training Officers and Other Ranks in Bayonet Fighting, to act as Instructors to their Battalions.

HAVERSACKS.
12. The Division is indenting for extra haversacks for carrying Rifle Grenades. These will have to be altered by Battalion Tailors for the purpose.

TRAINING OF A PLATOON.
13. The pamphlet issued by G.H.Q., on the subject is to be adhered to. The one variation will be the programme. The method and principles laid down should be regarded as F.S.R., All Commanding Officers should go through it carefully paragraph by paragraph with their Officers and emphasise all the important points. (Instructions for the Training of Platoons for Offensive Action).

RIFLEMEN.
14. There will be only 1 Section of Riflemen in a Platoon but every man must be thoroughly efficient in the use of Rifle and Bayonet which are the Infantry Man's first weapons. The remaining Sections will be made up - one of Bombers, one of Rifle Bombers, one of Lewis Gunners.

31st March 1917.

F. Beaumont-Nesbitt
Captain,
Brigade Major, 1st Guards Brigade.

Table of Trend Duty

	12	13	14	15	16	17	18	19	20	21	3	4	5	6	7	8	9	10	11	12	13	14	15	16	17	18	19	20	21	22	23	24	25	26	27	28	29	30	31
2nd Grenadier Gds						I									I											I				I						I			
2nd Coldstream Gds					I														I					I															
3rd Coldstream Gds													I									I							I										
1st Irish Gds				I												I											I												
1st Coldstream Gds										I							I									I													
2nd Irish Gds									I											I									I										

	Nov 12th to Jan 3rd 1917	10	11	12	13	14	15	16	17	18	19	20	21	22	23	24	25	26	27	28	Feb	12	13	14	15	16	17	18	19	20	21	22	23	24	25	26
2nd Grenadier Gds	11 nights																																			
2nd Coldstream Gds	13 nights					I																														
3rd Coldstream Gds	13 nights									I																										
1st Irish Gds	14 nights											I																								
1st Coldstream Gds	13 nights													I																						
2nd Irish Gds	10 nights															I																				

S E C R E T.   1st G.B. No. 119.

2nd Bn. Grenadier Guards.   Guards Division.
2nd Bn. Coldstream Guards.   75th Field Coy., R.E.
3rd Bn. Coldstream Guards.   4th Field Ambulance.
1st Bn. Irish Guards.
Bde., Machine Gun Company.
Bde., Trench Mortar Battery.

    1st Guards Brigade Hd-Qrs., will close tomorrow at BOIS DOUAGE at 5 p.m. and open at ARROWHEAD Copse (S.30.a.9.1.) at the same hour.

ACKNOWLEDGE.

26th March 1917.

                                                Captain,
                               Brigade Major, 1st Guards Brigade.

SECRET.   1st G.B. No.117.

Bde., Machine Gun Company.
Bde., Trench Mortar Battery.
2nd Bn. Grenadier Guards.
2nd Bn. Coldstream Guards.   ) (for information.)
3rd Bn. Coldstream Guards.
1st Bn. Irish Guards.

1.   1st Guards Brigade Machine Gun Company and Trench Mortar Battery will move tomorrow 27th inst., to LE TRANSLOY Area – O.25.a. – where they will be camped.

2.   The Machine Gun Company and Trench Mortar Battery will not pass E. of the BEAULENCOURT – SAILLY SAILLISEL Road before 3 p.m.

3.   Billeting parties will report to a representative of "Q" Branch, Guards Division, at N.30.b.8.5. at 12 noon.

4.   Machine Guns and Trench Mortars will be stored at MAUREPAS Camp and will be under the charge of the details left behind. O.C., Bde. Machine Gun Company and O.C., Bde. Trench Mortar Battery will communicate direct with Camp Commandant, MAUREPAS, concerning this.

5.   The C.R.E. Guards Division will issue instructions for work on the SOUTH COPSE Decauville Railway which will begin on March 28th.

6.   Administrative Orders G.D. No.797/40/A are attached.

ACKNOWLEDGE.

26th March 1917.   Captain.
                                                             Brigade Major, 1st Guards Brigade.

www.ingramcontent.com/pod-product-compliance
Lightning Source LLC
Chambersburg PA
CBHW081440160426

43193CB00013B/2336